BFI Modern Classics

Rob White
Series Editor

BFI Modern Classics is a series of critical studies of films produced over the last three decades. An array of writers explore their chosen films, offering a range of perspectives on the dominant art and entertainment medium in contemporary culture. The series gathers together snapshots of our passion for and understanding of recent movies.

Also Published

Do the Right Thing
Ed Guerrero

The Silence of the Lambs
Yvonne Tasker

Trainspotting
Murray Smith

(see a full list of titles in the series at the back of this book)

Forthcoming

City of Sadness
Berenice Reynaud

Dilwale Dulhaniya Le Jeyenge
Anupama Chopra

Eyes Wide Shut
Michel Chion

Heat
Nick James

Jaws
Antonia Quirke

LA Confidential
Manohla Dargis

The Matrix
Margaret Morse

Star Wars
Peter Wollen

The Usual Suspects

Ernest Larsen

bfi Publishing

For Nadja (so unusual, so unsuspected)

First published in 2002 by the
British Film Institute
21 Stephen Street, London W1T 1LN

The British Film Institute promotes greater
understanding and appreciation of,
and access to, film and moving image
culture in the UK.

British Library Cataloguing-in-Publication Data
A catalogue record for this book is available
from the British Library

ISBN 0-85170-869-2

Series design by Andrew Barron &
Collis Clements Associates

Typeset in Italian Garamond and Swiss 721BT
by D R Bungay Associates, Burghfield, Berks

Printed in Great Britain by
Norwich Colour Print, Drayton, Norfolk

Contents

Acknowledgments *6*

1 Off-screen, behind the Scenes *7*

2 Heist Noir *23*

3 On the Side of a Bus *53*

4 The Shattered Coffee-cup *75*

Notes *89*

Credits *91*

Acknowledgments

I am deeply grateful to Dana Polan, Toby Miller, and Marita Sturken for their unstinting support at crucial moments in the development of this study. Thanks are also due to Rob White, my editor, for his patient oversight of this project, and to Tom Cabot, for his meticulous production of the book. Sherry Millner's unique ability to combine vivid enthusiasm with critical acumen decisively moved me beyond more than a few bad patches. And finally, I should note the uncanny foresight Marc Siegal displayed a few years ago one fine spring night in Berlin by taking us to a wicked bar named Keyser Soze – at the intersection, that is, of cinema and intoxication.

1 Off-screen, behind the Scenes

Bryan Singer, who directed *The Usual Suspects*, prodded its scriptwriter Christopher McQuarrie to produce something like nine rewrites before he was satisfied that the story they'd developed was airtight. At the front of each version of the script, according to Singer, they 'put a quote from "Sympathy for the Devil": "Please allow me to introduce myself / hope you guess my name. But what is bothering you / is the nature of my game."'[1] In the scene that introduces the finished film just such a crucial guess is made. The rest of the film proceeds to spell out the nature of the game.

The first shot, following the credits and a title ('San Pedro, California – last night'), is an extreme close-up of an open matchbook set aflame. A cranked audio track makes the sudden flash sound like an

The opening conflagration

explosion. Cut. Dean Keaton (Gabriel Byrne), slumped on the deck of a boat, manages to light a last cigarette with the torched matchbook. Who knows why, but no tough guy is allowed to resist lighting up as the flame of his life is about to be snuffed out. In another offhand and therefore very cool gesture of despair, Keaton then ignites the trail of a fuse only inches away. The camera follows as the path of the moving flame skirts a corpse. Suddenly a stream of liquid douses the flame. The camera tilts up slowly and portentously to the bridge where an unidentifiable man, having pissed out the fire, is busy buttoning his fly. He's quite a marksman.

Since Singer has deliberately begun the scene (and the movie) at the point when the action is all but over, something other than mere action must be at stake. The mystery man approaches Keaton. Keaton looks up.

The moment of recognition

A light dawns in this stricken man's eyes. He says, 'Can't feel my legs …
Keyser', enunciating the name as if for the first time. His paralysis is set off
against this mysterious source of power, whose first name puns on Kaiser,
the king of kings. The last-second knowledge of the identity of Keyser
Soze that Keaton gains is, as it turns out, denied to us until the last
seconds of the film itself. The explosions and fires, the twenty-seven dead
bodies, the outbreaks and results of violence, are bracketed by the fact
that we can't see what Keaton sees as his life ebbs away.

Keyser Soze lights a cigarette, his face still off-screen. Only the most
impassive gunmen pause to light up before the act of movie murder. Using
his left hand, he pulls a gun out of his coat pocket. He lifts his arm. The
butt of the gun is horizontal as he shoots Keaton. Only the most
experienced gunmen commit murder with such style, such nonchalance.
He walks away, tossing the cigarette he's just lit onto the fuse without even
looking. Once again he hits the mark effortlessly. As he escapes, a series of
explosions turns the boat into a floating inferno. The game is on.

January, 1993. Snow is falling on the teeming streets of Park City, Utah,
site of the Sundance Film Festival. Christopher McQuarrie is standing in a
line outside a theatre waiting for a screening of *Public Access*, which he co-
wrote with his best friend, Bryan Singer, then only twenty-five years old.
Somebody asks about his next project. He says he has 'just seen a column
in *Spy* magazine called "The Usual Suspects" and I thought that would be

Impassive, nonchalant

a neat title for a movie'. What would the movie be about? 'Well', McQuarrie says, looking up at the sky as if the answer might be written there, 'it's called *The Usual Suspects*, so I guess it's about a bunch of criminals who meet in a police lineup.'[2] He then describes in detail this imaginary movie's poster – the image of a lineup. Creating a movie in the space between a neat title and a snappy poster is the stuff of B-movie legend. Both Roger Corman and his sometime producers, Jim Nicholson and Sam Arkoff of American-International, notoriously claimed to pre-sell exploitation flicks on that basis. McQuarrie's palpable glee in telling this anecdote suggests his strong attraction to the identity of an industry pro.

Singer and McQuarrie grew up together in the solidly middle-class, small town of Princeton Junction, New Jersey, which is less than two hours by car from New York City. Singer started making 8mm films when he was thirteen, with a camera borrowed from a friend. So formative was this experience that Singer says that his goal as an adult director 'is to move the entire crew and cameras with the same agility that I did with my 8mm camera as a boy'.[3] Following a stint at the School of Visual Arts in New York City, he transferred to the University of Southern California – majoring in film history, not film-making. After graduation he quickly made a short 16mm film on borrowed money, about six high-school friends who meet six months after their graduation and realise they are no longer so close. Called *Lion's Den*, it starred another boyhood friend,

The lineup

Ethan Hawke. Then, with still another friend, John Ottman, in the dual role of editor and composer, they made *Public Access*, which went on to become co-winner of the grand prize at Sundance.

McQuarrie soon began developing the script for *The Usual Suspects*, but found there wasn't enough narrative juice to be squeezed from just a title and an image. So he did what screenwriters always do. He stole – not, however, from someone else but from himself, revamping an idea from one of his own unproduced scripts.

What he'd started with was a variation on the heist movie, a noir sub-genre, epitomised by John Huston's *The Asphalt Jungle* (1950) and fervidly updated by Quentin Tarantino's *Reservoir Dogs* (1992). That was good but wasn't enough. In heist movies a bunch of tough but fairly desperate professional crooks get together in the big ugly city and plan one last big score and come as close as you can get to putting it over before everything goes haywire. The variant that McQuarrie had come up with deliberately discarded one key element of the classic scenario: the role of the mastermind. The usual suspects are not – it appears – drawn together by the initiative and brilliance of the criminal mastermind. They're sitting around fuming in a holding cell and spontaneously decide to take revenge on the cops, a moment of democratic resentment that gives McQuarrie's premise an initial edge.

The idea that McQuarrie lifted from his own back pocket was the story of a man who cold-bloodedly murders his own family and calmly walks away, disappearing from view. (*Public Access*, it's worth noting, involves the story of a strange young man who wanders into an ordinary suburban town – not unlike Princeton Junction, one suspects – and, apparently without motivation, murders several of its citizens before calmly walking away.) In returning to the idea of the killer Dad, McQuarrie eventually found himself smuggling back into the script the mastermind his initial premise had dispensed with. But at the same time he didn't want to squander the energy implicit in the idea of the self-motivated team of crooks – so this mastermind character somehow had to be mated with that premise. His heist narrative, with its distinctively urban realism, is crossed now with a completely different kind of crime story based in the twisted dynamics of a

classically patriarchal nuclear family. McQuarrie made up the heist story and along the way carefully adorned it with credible detail. But he didn't make up the much more sensational family massacre. He knew that story as well as he knew the back of his hand.

On 9 November 1971, in the affluent town of Westfield, New Jersey, John List, a mild-mannered, devoutly Lutheran accountant, murdered his wife, his mother and his three teenage children. He wrote a series of rambling kiss-off letters on a memo pad labelled 'A Few Words from John E. List, Career-Builder'.[4] Attesting to massive debts, and to his feeling that he wasn't enough of a man, he considered that his murdered family was best left to God's care in heaven. His pastor, he wrote, was the one person who would 'understand'. And finally: 'P. S. Mother is in the hallway in the attic – 3rd floor. She was too heavy to move.'[5] Leaving his nineteen-room mansion behind along with the five bloody bodies, he disappeared. He lived for the next eighteen years as freely as anybody who's murdered his family could be said to live. Finally, a popular television show, *America's Most Wanted*, hired forensic sculptor Frank Bender to create a bust that, combining scientific and artistic techniques, would show what John List might look like in 1989. After airing a story on what was billed as 'the most infamous murder case in the history of New Jersey',[6] focusing fifteen million eyes on the case, the producers received more than 200 tips. It's unclear whether List, who was an avid fan of the show, saw that week's episode or not. On 1 June 1989, John List, remarried and working as an accountant under the alias Robert Clark, was arrested in Richmond, Virginia. Extradited, tried and convicted, he was sentenced to five consecutive life sentences. *The Usual Suspects* was not the first film to take up this grisly story. In 1993, *Judgment Day: The John List Story*, directed by Bobby Roth, appeared. The film starred Robert Blake in the lead role, a fact which takes on a bizarre twist, given that seven years later Blake's own wife was murdered, with Blake himself considered a prime suspect, at least in the media, though charges were never proffered.

Both McQuarrie and Singer were born and raised only a hop, skip and a jump from Westfield, from the all too real scene in which this middle-class Dad, a Cub Scout leader and Sunday-school teacher, who seemed as normal as their own fathers, went ape. McQuarrie (who was three years old when the murders occurred) attempts to find some saving grace in this suburban conjunction of banality and violence:

> my guess was that he didn't want his family to experience poverty … I think that in some twisted way, he really felt like he was saving his family a lot of misery by killing them. And when they finally prosecuted him, that was his defense: that he was being merciful to his family. So that really sort of stuck in my craw. I had the idea for a character who murders his own family long before this script ever existed.[7]

In the end, McQuarrie and Singer go through some major gyrations to get the disturbing reality of the List massacre to do what they want it to do in a script heavily invested in twisting genre conventions. They invert nearly

Robert Blake starring in *In Cold Blood* (Richard Brooks, 1967)

every aspect of that reality – except its determining influence. The suburbanite who's too much of a coward to face up to his own failure is an utterly commonplace figure. This particular one, John List, seems exceptional in only one way: he lived in such a fantasy world that he could justify murdering his own family.

The task McQuarrie and Singer set themselves is to reimagine the circumstances of such an intimately repulsive, peculiarly primal crime. What they choose to do is to distance that palpable threat. They exoticise the haunting story, relocating the murders to Hungary and naming the perpetrator Keyser Soze. Instead of a pathetically weak nobody hiding behind God, their character is a mythically ruthless, global criminal mastermind who in the defining moment of his career is, in McQuarrie's words:

put in a situation where someone's going to kill his family, so he does it instead. And it's a lot quicker and a lot less painful. And of course, with Keyser, it destroys him. His family was all he had, and now he is this utterly ruthless shell of a man. I really believe that you're not born that ruthless and that evil and that cunning and that cold; you're made that way. And I think that an incident like that could make him that way. It's not that he hates anybody in particular – he's mad at life, life really screwed him. Ultimately, like every other character in the script, he really brought it on himself. He's gotten mixed up in a bad business. And everybody in the script, I think – whether they indicate it or not – understands from the beginning that this is the business they've chosen. They don't blame Keyser for killing them, that's just the way it works.[8]

Like the good accountant he was, List planned his murders well ahead of time and in meticulous detail. In no way were they the product of an impulsive decision, a split-second assertion of male wilfulness and power and a refusal to buckle under to pressure or to one's deadly enemies, whoever they might be. List felt that he couldn't bear the pressure of not being enough of a man. Singer and McQuarrie invert this failure of manhood in *The Usual Suspects*. Their murderous father now represents the

A yellow-tinted nightmare

Young Soze's gun

The spook spooking himself

outer limits of what a man can be forced to do to *affirm* his manhood, taking control no matter what the cost. This affirmation of male ruthlessness becomes the secret and the motor of Keyser Soze's spectacular success – as well as providing a way for McQuarrie to fuse what would initially seem like two warring genres in his effort to remodel the script.

List became Soze. A horrifying scene of domestic violence became a mythical act of murderous self-assertion. Smalltown America became middle Europe, redolent for American audiences of medieval barbarism, pogroms, the madness of ethnic cleansing. In a flashback during his interrogation by Detective Dave Kujan (Chazz Palminteri) – a flashback that is more logical than it first seems – Verbal Kint (Kevin Spacey), palsied survivor of the shoreside carnage shown in the opening minutes, conjures up the legendary turning point of Keyser Soze's life. Refusing to be blackmailed by men who have entered his home and taken his wife and children as hostages, Soze chooses to shoot them himself, then the intruders – and later to wreak a fuller vengeance on *their* families.

Filmed as a smeary, yellow-tinted, overexposed, slo-mo nightmare of gunplay and incineration, the massacre is far more visually stylised than any other scene in a movie replete with violent action: it is in utter contrast to the realist *mise en scène* of the rest of the film. Singer emphatically distinguishes between the two kinds of violence. The preternatural horror provoked by the domestic murder scene far outstrips the adult male-on-male violence of the rest of the film, which is much more deeply rooted in genre conventions. Since it's portrayed so differently and so contained within the airtight capsule of long ago and far away, it's as if we're looking at a scene from another movie. Furthermore, Singer's use of slow-motion, soft-focus hand-held pans masks the specific physical identity of the strangely long-haired perpetrator and his stunned victims, a ploy that generalises the horror of the abject dependency of the family upon the unleashed father. Coded with the traumatic presence of a repeated nightmare, the scene pulses with a vehemence that all but ruptures the narrative flow. Looking respectfully terrror-stricken, Verbal ups the ante even further by referring to Soze as the incarnation of the devil. (For this, McQuarrie may be transposing certain notorious details garnishing the

List carnage: List's daughter Pat dabbled in witchcraft; shortly after the crime the List mansion, Breeze Knoll, became the favourite midnight haunt of teenage Satanists; and nine months after the genteel massacre, an arsonist torched the place.[9]) When bundled with the cultivation of threatening exoticism and the vividly excessive staging, Verbal's credulous identification of occult (i.e. deregulated) evil abroad on a global scale wrenches the crime drama loose from its recognisable moorings, setting it frighteningly adrift in an even darker underworld. As List drove out of Westfield on the night of the murders, he passed the Rialto theatre, where the revenge movie, *Billy Jack* (Tom Laughlin, 1971), was playing. The poster outside described it as the story of 'a person who protects children and other living things'.[10]

In leaving the question of Keyser Soze's identity unsettled until the very end, Singer and McQuarrie also effectively exacerbate the ultimate question of the location of power. Their apparent intuition that power may not be localisable, or at the very least that it is so ceaselessly mobile that you can never assuredly point your finger directly at it, is given additional credibility by the profile they supply their villain Soze. He personifies, in the mid-90s, a new, unstable Europe, which was riven both by tribal war and by organised crime. A post-communist era, Eastern European rogue

The release poster for
Billy Jack

international arms dealer resonated with a virtual deluge of news stories at the time about the rampant influence of such brazen princes of crime, who, we were told, operate with impunity and mercilessly punish every affront with savage violence. Such stories often began by depicting post-communist societies in a state of near-chaos and ended up covertly glamorising the shadowy figures they set out to pillory. The implication is that these potentates are horrible but that, not unlike the robber barons of end-of-the-century industrial United States, they sure as hell know how to make cut-throat capitalism work for them. In *The Usual Suspects* the frisson of deregulated terror that strikes characters whenever the dreaded name of Soze is uttered has been earned in advance by other real-life tough guys whose foreign-looking names we're not sure how to pronounce.

That said, the virtually all-powerful, international criminal mastermind, who secretly and invisibly controls nearly everything that happens, has, in fact, numberless precedents in movie serials and comic books. A similar figure appears in Fritz Lang's first two Dr Mabuse films. Mabuse is a specialist in disguise, mind-control, hypnotism and gambling, who delightedly wreaks havoc on a virtually defenceless society until finally he goes insane. As Kracauer says of the first Mabuse film, it 'succeeds in making of Mabuse an omnipresent threat which cannot be localized, and thus reflects society under a tyrannical regime – that kind of society in which one fears everybody because anybody may be the tyrant's ear or

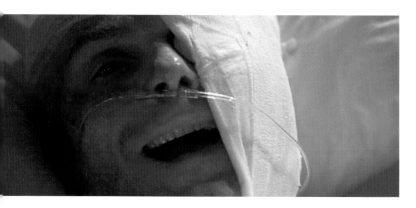

The Hungarian survivor: 'Keyser Soze!'

Dr Mabuse and his deck of identities

arm'.[11] Since, however, unlike Soze, Mabuse appears to operate on a national rather than a global scale, he focuses the shifting relations between irrationality and social control on the dynamics of German society, playing out a national psychic conflict, it's often argued, between the fear of and the desire for totalitarianism. His nefarious schemes thus occupy centre stage, while Soze is evident only in the results he produces from a distance. Working behind the scenes of the global stage, the object of rumour and innuendo, but never pinned down with actual fact, Soze is a far hazier entity rhetorically associated with the occult. As Verbal says of him, 'the greatest trick the Devil ever pulled, was convincing the world he didn't exist.' With the film-makers deliberately keeping us in the dark about him, the further we get into the film the more Soze takes on the gloomy aura of the Prince of Darkness.

The super-villain is also familiar from comic books. However, in comics such a figure functions as a foil who demonstrates the ultimate invincibility of the superhero (nowhere to be found in *The Usual Suspects*). The paradigmatic consumer of this combat has always been the powerless child, most often an adolescent or pre-adolescent male, engaged in a daily if not minute-by-minute struggle against the oppressive adult world. For the child, such comics satisfyingly portray scenarios seething with rage, violence, rebellion, fear, anxiety – and victory. Singer's interest in this psychology became obvious in the two

Ian McKellen in *Apt Pupil*

films he made after *The Usual Suspects*. *Apt Pupil* (1998) dramatises a smart suburban teen's perverse attraction to authoritarianism when he discovers that a neighbourhood recluse is actually a Nazi in hiding. The disturbing scene in which the kid (smallish Brad Renfro) forces the old Nazi (towering Ian McKellen) to don SS drag and goosestep around his dishevelled bungalow heatedly displays a dynamic of homoerotic sadomasochism with the usual roles of subject and master, child and adult, reversed and discreetly desublimated.

Singer's adapation of the comic book series *X-Men* (2000) begins with a sketchy historical evocation of Nazism and then spells out how its tormented young characters experience their 'superpowers' as afflictions that ostracise them from everything they know and love. The best scenes transform the physical and emotional tremors of adolescent sexuality into dangerous mutations as Singer gets full value for his newly found access to costly special effects. These effects also maximise the efficacy of disguise by playing with the impossibility of telling the difference between mutant and non-mutant. Effects that a magus like Mabuse could only have dreamed about have become an everyday task for post-production giants like Industrial Light & Magic. In the end, however, the accumulation of effects in *X-Men* drowns out the narrative. The kids eventually achieve some sort of salvation or respite through rousing bouts of team violence – which is also how *The Usual Suspects* works through or around the problem that active sexuality seems to represent for its characters. All three films strikingly locate the deep source of the evil that afflicts its characters as a menace presently hidden in the heart of American society that has somehow migrated from bad old Europe.

In this expanded context, the evil mastermind trope should not be dismissed as mere kids' stuff. Its deployment in *The Usual Suspects* is in the end at least as 'realistic' emotionally for McQuarrie and Singer as the original premise of the heist movie. Just as they are haunted by the John List story, as New Jersey kids who were consumers of comic book adventure narratives, so the film is haunted by the film-makers' fascination with List. His double, Soze, is not really 'in' the film: he haunts it, a structuring absence glimpsed only fleetingly in flashback and at the end. For the rest, Singer uses off-screen space to evoke his terrible presence or we hear his name uttered as a rumour, a legend, a curse, a source of absolute terror.

This strategy of absence renovates certain motifs common to American movie serials of the late 30s and early 40s. In these fragmented mini-narratives it was often a matter of considerable uncertainty whether the criminal mastermind, usually a master of disguise like Mabuse, was really present in a given scene or not – until the very last moment, when he was typically unmasked as the hero's faithful friend or selfless benefactor. Otherwise, at the point of violence, this arch villain would typically become the fearsome object of a gaze off-screen or would become visible only as an approaching silhouette holding a dagger on high or an outstretched pistol. But the silhouette, the off-screen gaze, the disguise and the misrecognition, all of them more theatrical in origin than specifically cinematic, are just as effective with adults as I remember them being in the Saturday afternoon matinees I attended as a kid at the Gateway theatre in Chicago. In *The Usual Suspects*, the elaborate play on absence, reference and invisibility produces an increasingly dense atmosphere of pervasive menace. As a result, the name Keyser Soze seems to apply less to an actual person than to a force, thereby transforming the endlessly deferred answer to the plot question of the villain's identity into the more disturbing question of what Keyser Soze represents.

Verbal invokes the rumour of Keyser Soze

2 Heist Noir

The film does not defer answering the question of who the usual suspects are. One of two survivors of the shipboard debacle, Verbal Kint, testifies largely in voiceover to how the usual suspects got together. Via chronological flashbacks that begin, he says, just six weeks earlier, it takes four scenes to get there: the roundup, the lineup, the grilling and the wait in the holding cell. Shooting in a speedy shorthand with a liberal salting of jump-cuts, Singer edits the roundup and the grilling to highlight parallels among the suspects, visually situating them as equals. In both the lineup and the holding-cell scenes, he allows his actors some room to strut.

One by one each suspect is rounded up. The comically belligerent McManus (Stephen Baldwin) is rousted out of his bed, irritably cynical Todd Hockney (Kevin Pollak) from his garage, perpetually incoherent Fenster (Benicio del Toro) from the street, and the anxiously reflective Keaton from an upmarket restaurant. Each of the suspects is sketched in terms of physical type and attitude, but Singer shoots the police as an undifferentiated gang. Until they get to Keaton: because with him it's personal. The customs officer Dave Kujan drags Keaton away while he's huddled with his lawyer girlfriend Edie Finneran (Suzy Amis), making a pitch to a pair of Frenchmen to secure financial backing for a restaurant. The scene sets up Keaton as the only suspect with even half a hankering to go straight.

Keaton arrested

When the bunch of criminals meet in the lineup, Singer encourages his actors to play for comic bravado. Each suspect is compelled by the police on the other side of the one-way mirror to repeat in turn the mellifluous line, 'Hand me the keys, you fucking cocksucker.' Filled with contempt for the police, the suspects begin to goof on the line, torturing its profane absurdity. They're like ham actors at an audition, which is more or less what a lineup amounts to, a tryout for the drama of the trial.

The set is decorated with severe simplicity, its rigid horizontality emphasised by black height lines printed on the white backdrop. The suspected felons come on stage, Verbal leading the way. Singer coolly shoots his bad leg in a low-angle close-up. By now it's clear how much Singer loves close-ups. He loves them so much that many shots start in close-up and then almost unobtrusively move in even closer. The lights go up. The first suspect, the compact Todd Hockney, with his fuck-you stare, is asked to read the words written on a piece of paper he holds in his hand. He does so as if it's beneath his dignity even to comment. He passes the slip of paper to the wise guy McManus. McManus mockingly overemotes the line but nobody laughs. The cops order him to knock it off. The third suspect, the beanpole Fenster, manages to crack everybody up with his off-beat mumbling.

During production the actors were never able to complete any takes of this scene as scripted without breaking up. While editing, Singer made use of their unrehearsed spontaneous energy to give the scene its edge. As

Comic defiance

Only a gimp

the most relaxed scene in the film – come to think of it, the only relaxed
scene – its improvisatory mood quickly suggests the beginnings of group
camaraderie. Fenster slaps McManus on the arm and McManus returns
the punch. Clearly they already know each other. Next, Keaton glances
down to avoid laughing out loud. Singer has cut to medium shot to
capture the body language. Fenster garbles the line masterfully. In a fury,
the cops order him to speak English. Nudged by Singer's inclusive
framing we begin to perceive the suspects as members of a team-in-the-
making, each with his own defining traits. Hockney, a trained mechanic,
evinces fierce, functional self-containment, a touchy disdain for emotional
involvement and an eye for detail. The muscular McManus, a boyish but

The most relaxed moment in the film

aggressive show-off, compensates for his emotional immaturity with a carefully trimmed beard. Fenster, oddball inventor and sole native speaker of para-English, wears a red shirt left unbuttoned to expose his hairless chest. They come across, first and foremost, as tough, competitive, suspicious young men, full of attitude and already showing enough rapport to play off each other. Every young man in the audience is supposed to be imagining himself up there, slouching, squinting, saying, 'you fucking cocksucker' to the cops and getting away with it.

The lineup scene has always had a basically ritualistic character, the object of which is to enact that awful moment when the innocent witness/victim is supposed to finger the guilty man. Suspense is sustained by the precise length of a point-of-view shot, a slow pan from left to right, as the anxious victim seeks out the tormentor. While at most only one suspect could possibly be guilty, invariably they all look like crooks. In rituals, context dictates perception. But just as the suspects comically rebel against the role of submissive criminal scripted for them by the police, so the film-makers tellingly reject the obligatory moment of identification by omitting the victim's role altogether. The police are after the hijackers of a truck full of gun parts, but the truck driver isn't there to point the finger – nor to listen to the suspects read that goofy line. That means there was no point in asking them to read it in the first place. There is no pan, no point-of-view shot, no innocent gaze. The scene is staged with the dramatic point of the ritual missing. With the victim absent, the privilege ritually accorded the legal system is mocked, if not undermined. The police act as if the suspects must all be guilty of the hijacking. But, for the moment, they don't seem to be guilty of much more than the crime of being alive.

The suspects are unstintingly defiant in this scene and, even more emphatically, in the following scene in which they are grilled, one by one. They dare the authorities to do their damnedest, which is what we expect tough guys to do. The two scenes establish that, if they weren't trapped, they'd be nervy enough to take action, to contest the capricious character of the rule of law.

The scene (five short scenes edited as a set-piece) in which the five suspects are grilled, one at a time, is shot entirely from the same theatrical straight-into-the-camera angle, with the same high-key overhead lighting, each suspect in the centre of the frame, with overlapping dialogue and more jump-cuts on the action. To seal the deal of the suspects' equality, the cops, their faces almost entirely cropped out of the tight medium close-up, prowl around each tormented but defiant suspect, who faces forward except when being slapped around. The fifth, Keaton, is subjected to the worst violence. The cops regard him with utter contempt and only later do we find out why: he's a bent cop, drummed out of the force years earlier for corruption. It's smart to stage this sequence as the third of the four scenes, following rather than preceding the lineup. With each of the suspects isolated, we feel how dramatically their vulnerability as individuals is heightened. However, none of them shows any sign of weakening. The film-makers' strategy of denying the cops even the least grace note of individuality abstracts them into willing representatives of a cruel system. The suspects begin to look like the best kind of victims: the kind that courageously refuses to be victimised.

In the holding cell the men are together again and, though they're still in custody, rebellion is taking over from defiance. It's a tricky scene dramatically and somewhat less intense visually considering the impact of the previous three formally much more rigorous scenes. At first, it just seems to be about how trapped men jockey for ascendancy. The suspects, having all endured lavish humiliation, have things to say to each other. Singer blocks the scene so that McManus, Fenster and Hockney embody

Grilled by undifferentiated cops

one faction in the cell, screen right. McManus moves diagonally across the space, screen left, to taunt Keaton, before backing off. Keaton and Verbal maintain their physical distance from the other three – but then the latter, without moving from his place apart, attempts to make common cause with the trio. He wants to belong, we realise. The trio takes the lead in imagining a plausible revenge on the cops – not just these particular cops, but the system as a whole. They're after bigger game. They've been the hunted and now they want to become the hunters. To do that they must become a team. All five of them have to be in on it.

It seems implausible at first. One camera movement, a pan left from the trio to Verbal sitting alone in the background, seems to gauge the impact of his physical difference. McManus says, 'What about the gimp?' McManus, Hockney and Fenster have been alternating bluffs, threats, threatening movements and a strikingly flirtatious outpouring of homophobic jibes. In relation to this display of aggression, Verbal remains something of an ambiguous anomaly. Would they even accept him? Keaton meanwhile is holding out. The casting of Gabriel Byrne against type – his romantic black Irish looks and angst-ridden glower seem distinctly not usual suspect material – pays off here. Singer says that Byrne's face 'has just the right number of flaws to make it beautiful'.[12] This early in the film – with his showy and mysterious death scene still exerting its pull, with the extra weight given to his scene in the restaurant, and now with all the energy of this scene keyed to his decision – we are thinking his might be the star role.

The 'pretzel man' still isolated

It falls to the weakest of the suspects, Verbal, to clinch the issue of making the usual suspects into a team. This is a nice touch, and it becomes an even nicer touch later when things turn out to be not what they seem. What's pleasing the first time is that it makes a lot of sense that the weakest person has the strongest motivation, the most to gain. Verbal, at this point claiming to be 'the man with the plan', attempts to persuade the reluctant Keaton to take part in the plan to rip off the corrupt New York City cops who are running a smuggler's escort service right out of the blue and white cop cars – a profitably illegal operation known to the cognoscenti as New York's Finest Taxi Service. Spacey plays the scene with a masochism that would provoke a saint. Getting Keaton to hit him, Verbal plays the crippled and now injured victim for all it's worth.

Singer shoots the first part of the scene in medium close-up, then cuts unexpectedly to the establishing shot of Edie's modern, open-plan, split-level Park Avenue apartment, sporting Italian designer furniture and a faux-Morris Louis abstract painting on the far wall. (This is about the only domestic space we see in the whole film.) Ostentatiously nursing his pain – 'I'll shit blood in the morning' – Verbal avoids going anywhere near the furniture, perching instead on the steps leading down to the next level. He looks like he's crossed into alien territory. His discomfort in this antiseptically chic space broadly hints at a rift between classes. Saying nothing, Keaton nevertheless signifies his agreement to the plan by sitting down next to Verbal. Maybe he's beginning to realise that he doesn't quite

Alienated by modernism

belong in this world either. Without saying a word, the two men appear to establish a basic level of understanding. Keaton's body language is eloquent: he has to go along now. He really doesn't have any other option, except to become increasingly dependent on Edie. The dialogue in this scene scarcely matters. Both Verbal and Keaton speak through their physical movements – appropriate for men who come into their own in the midst of action.

The usual suspects, in choosing to move from foul-mouthed defiance to active rebellion against the cops, find themselves taking on and fulfilling the police suspicions of them. Singer and McQuarrie pause for a detailed account of Keaton's waffling before becoming part of the team. His role is pivotal in undermining the importance of the individual in favour of the anti-star configuration of the team. Verbal convinces Keaton that he must give up his individualism – and his girlfriend Edie – in order to regain his dignity. Keaton's anguished decision to sacrifice his affective connection foreshadows Keyser Soze's instantaneous decision literally to sacrifice his family. In both cases, the character affirms his manhood by denying such connection. If Soze's fierce insistence on autonomy is radically nihilistic, with Keaton's decision individual psychology gives way to group psychology. However, we are already in a position of knowing that this embrace of the team ends disastrously for Keaton – and the others. Which leaves us wondering about the value or the validity of the team as an alternative to going it alone.

'The usual suspects' count as the reserve army of all-but-anonymous stand-ins regarded by the police as capable of any crime currently claiming their attention. In film, they're the 'extras' of the cinematic judicial system who, in the lineup, flank either the one who did it (Tony Curtis in *The Boston Strangler*, 1968) or the one mistakenly picked out as the culprit (Henry Fonda in *The Wrong Man*, 1957). They are the objects of that gaze which pans over them (slowly, in medium close-up) with comparative indifference, since they are only ordinary petty criminals and not *the* criminal, the one who matters. In most films, the usual suspects seldom have speaking parts and thus, as the most minor of minor characters, are slated neither for heroism nor villainy. Since they can neither rise nor fall, since they are irrelevantly both innocent and guilty, they appear to be so undramatic, so close to invisible, that they recede into the wallpaper. Singer and McQuarrie capitalise on this logic, the most vulnerable aspect of which lies in the fact that most of us, routinely prone to identifying ourselves as both innocent and guilty in our everyday lives, could be fairly described as usual suspects. Furthermore, Singer and McQuarrie discovered that when the suspects became a team they shed the narrative inertia of their roles as place markers, moving from the dim sidelines to the burnished centre of the terrain of cinematic stories about collective male aggression – crime stories, in other words.

The concept of 'the usual suspects' has not remained stable since its introduction in the form of an order briskly uttered by Claude Rains in his role as Vichy police captain Louis Renaud in Michael Curtiz's *Casablanca* (1942): 'Major Strasser has been shot. Round up the usual suspects.' The film's ever-expanding postwar popularity led eventually to the concept's widespread use as a sometimes ironic catchphrase that no longer referred to a selected group of likely criminals but in a vaguely ironic way described any pre-selected group with which one was familiar or overfamiliar. However, what in *Casablanca* had been a throwaway line referring to a previously unnamed, or at least publicly unnoted, category of human beings became in *The Usual Suspects* the focus. So marginal are 'the usual

Casablanca

suspects' in *Casablanca* that they remain off-screen and invisible. The film ends before anybody can be rounded up.

In *Casablanca* Rains plays a witty collaborator who, at the last moment, wises up and refuses to cooperate with the Nazis and thereby redeems himself. Singer's usual suspects refuse to knuckle under to a corrupt social order (the police) and in the end are destroyed (with one crucial exception). But there's a twist. Having exorcised the threat posed by female sexuality, with Keaton's sacrifice of Edie, the suspects are not wiped out by the police and neither do they self-destruct under pressure, which is how the previous films of this genre – heist noir – tended to finish.[13] While writing the script, McQuarrie came up with a third possibility, which led him to expand on his original premise. The usual suspects escape the domination of the system only to find that they have from the first been manipulated and dominated by a shadowy and malevolent mastermind who is even more powerful and far-reaching than the legal system against which they originally rebelled. The founding principle of the usual suspects, the principle of autonomous teamwork, turns out to be an enabling deception.

McQuarrie clearly likes to tell the how-*The Usual Suspects*-all-came-together story to valorise speed, spontaneity, serendipity and surprise – an ensemble of tactics that also applies to the film itself. Singer keeps the film running at a breakneck visual pace and likes to introduce plot twists on the wing with scant preparation, little screen time wasted on exposition, barely a look or a gesture that is not wired into the engine of the plot. As Singer says, 'the story is everything; every scene, image, every line, every sound effect has to be related to something else in the story. That detail, I think is the film's most gratifying thing.'[14] Not coincidentally, the usual suspects as a criminal team also display no taste for waste. This disciplined convergence of narrative form, expressive style and characterisation is as goal-directed as a guerrilla attack or a hunt. The film's action boils down to a series of hunts in which a team of men set out to entrap and often to kill, another team of men. The quarry is sighted, the team of hunters closes in to prevent escape, the quarry struggles, the hunters pitilessly dispose of their prey. Perhaps the cardinal principle of the hunt is never to let your quarry know that it is quarry: it's imperative never to neglect the element of surprise. In the end, the film springs its biggest surprise on the most vulnerable group of all: the audience.

The visceral excitement of the hunt is evoked with bravura outbursts of unpredictable violence in three action scenes: the NYPD heist, a jewellery robbery and an abortive effort to force their way free of Keyser Soze's henchmen in a highrise. Singer captures the atmospherically amoral beauty of anything-goes, high-testosterone risk-taking. The suspects come fully alive only when they are on the hunt. The rest of the time – brief but relatively talky scenes between longer action sequences – they seem to skulk or pose like a pack of young hounds in a kennel. Singer appreciates this oddly feral disposal of energy in the male body. He uses Pollak, del Toro and especially the sleek, muscular, bearded Baldwin (who moves with the grace of a seal in water) more often as animal presences than as complex characters. These memoryless creatures occupy only the present. Their strongest emotions – hatred and contempt – flare early on when they are themselves the abused objects of the police.

In the first heist scene, with all the suspects in black clothes and stocking masks, Singer combines rapid cutting, swish pans, hand-held camerawork and unexpected point-of-view shots to make it difficult to identify who's who at first. He exploits the visual intensity of the point where confusion and excitement jostle against each other like sticks of dynamite. The suspects, trailing a dapper jewel smuggler (Paul Bartel) picked up at the airport by the New York Police Department's blue and white, jam into position on a residential street, blocking the cop car back, front and left and right with their vans. The bewildered victims are trapped in every possible direction. While shouted threats pour down on the victims, McManus takes a sledge hammer to the windshield. With the camera placed in the car, the two stunned cops in the front seat cringe as McManus, who's dropped the sledge hammer by now, rips out the windshield in one piece. 'Good afternoon, my little pork chops', McManus calls out gleefully to the overweight pair.

The unblinking nerviness of the suspects' violence – its excessiveness from every direction – effectively paralyses the victims. The

'Good afternoon, my little pork chops'

scene adds comic fizz to the unremitting violence. The suspects' aims
(emeralds, the smuggler's cash payoff to the cops, exemplary revenge, 'a
little fuck-you to the NYPD from the five of us') achieved, McManus
douses the car with gasoline and insouciantly tosses his lighter onto the
roof of the still-occupied blue and white (a shot that teasingly recalls
Soze's tossed cigarette in the first scene). Verbal's voiceover reveals that,
thanks to Keaton, fifty-two corrupt cops were caught, including many
higher-ranking ones. 'Everybody got it right in the ass, from the chief on
down', he says reverently. Nothing could be more gratifying than a revenge
that compacts sexuality, violence and power into a single image violating
the cops' manhood. Only at this point, as the scene draws to an end, does

An ironic reference to Soze in the first scene

Singer cut to a master shot, the victims staggering out of the vehicular inferno.

Singer slows the pace of the action only once – at the decisive moment when the suspects raucously demand their booty, and the three victims briefly offer token resistance to their attackers' demands. This pause allows just enough room for the audience to participate imaginatively in answering an essential question while savouring the righteous sadism of the confrontation. Will the scene end in a killing? If the victims fail to come across, the suspects will shoot them. But it is clear that Singer wants the scene to argue for the justice of the revenge the suspects seek. His technical problem is how to stage such a scene with visual conviction that stops short of a blood-soaked confrontation. In fact, what's imaginative about the scene is its fierce deployment of the festive resources of verbal and gestural abandon: masquerade, trickery, cursing, the temporary reversal of customary power relations. One funny shot in this vein works as a casual marker of the suspects' ability to remain cool in action: a quick cut to Fenster with a cigarette jutting incongruously out of his masked lips, as if he's long been accustomed to smoke with a stocking over his head.

In the film's first action sequence revenge is focused; it stops short of murder. But in the next set-piece we see the unpredictability of violence, what happens when things start to get out of control. Once again jewels are the object, but the jewels are eventually revealed to be

'Everybody got it in the ass, from the chief on down'

unwanted bags of cocaine. In the first heist the comic/violent spirit of revenge decisively displaced the supposed object of desire, the emeralds. It was really the dirty cops who had to be snagged. The next action scene is as weakly motivated as the first heist seethed with revenge. The suspects decide to go 'back to work' because they have the opportunity to do so, and that's what suspects are supposed to do, or so Verbal's voiceover intimates. What turns out to matter here is the ability to seize the moment when everything's going wrong.

The justified strength of their desire for revenge in the first heist seemed to make the suspects invincible. This time the routine side of their attachment to danger makes them vulnerable. Once again there are three hoods on the other team. Singer locates the action in a strange and yet familiar urban site. For the second time, it's a place of transit and transition: an underground parking lot. A right-to-left pan picks up the other team walking toward their car and then in the foreground McManus's back as he stands over the open hood of a car, as if repairing it. His hand swings into view. He's holding a gun. The pan continues and picks up Hockney and Fenster on their way down a short ramp. They are talking boisterously, as if oblivious to their surroundings. They are disguised, wearing hats and dark glasses, and Fenster's arm is in a sling from which he pulls a gun, as a white van driven by Keaton powers down the ramp behind them. In a single shot Singer has precisely placed all the figures as they traverse the space. All the suspects turn out to be disguised, at a minimum wearing dark glasses. Keaton's dime-store black eye mask makes him look like a comic book superhero. But this disguise serves only to highlight his non-heroic failures of resolve and concentration at two key moments, failures that compromise the others.

The action speedily splits the characters into three areas of the garage. Keaton follows one bad guy who has jumped into his car. He smashes the driver's side window with a tyre iron and demands the case the guy has already stowed away, apparently the case that contains the jewels. But Keaton allows himself to be distracted at the wrong moment and the driver pulls a gun. They struggle. The gun fires. A car alarm starts squealing. In the confusion, the two bad guys overcome Fenster and Hockney. Everything's going wrong. Once again McManus becomes the figure who expresses the forbidden pleasure of uninhibited but highly competent aggression: a pistol in each fist, he swings left and right, right and left, in the effort to get two bad guys in his sights at the same time. Singer swings the camera back and forth in a point-of-view shot between the two big guys smothering Hockney and Fenster. McManus settles on an angle, and so does the camera. He shoots both guns at once. The two bad guys, blown back against the van, simultaneously release their grip on Hockney and Fenster. In unison they slide down the side of the white van, leaving behind twin smears of blood.

Then, as in the first heist, Singer slows down the action at a decisive moment. Keaton unexpectedly lacks sufficient resolve to despatch the third man, still behind the driver's seat. He stands there unable to pull the

Mark of efficiency

Gimp to the rescue

trigger. The example of McManus's energetic élan has been wasted on him. Such last-second displays of moral paralysis have a very long history in crime movies – but Keaton, we've been told, is a murderously tough customer. Finally, a shot rings out – but not from Keaton's gun. The framing shifts and we see Verbal, who has not been visible until that moment, holding a pistol. Singer's final pan, also right to left, follows Verbal but holds in close-up on the guy behind the steering wheel. There's a small red splotch squarely in the centre of his forehead; he's definitely staring at the beyond. So Keaton couldn't cut the mustard while the pathetic cripple Verbal turns out to be as cool as a cucumber (in dark glasses).

When things go wrong the team sticks together, compensating for each other's weaknesses. There's a cut to the white van parked near a cliff. The case is prised open. No jewels. In every respect this second scene has erased what the previous action scene gained: no treasure, no pride, no claim to social relevance – and three people no longer breathing on account of that parade of negatives. This reversal skirts futility when the suspects decide to confront Redfoot, the fence for the emeralds who set them up for this job. Their furious demand for satisfaction from Redfoot and his entourage of well-armed hoods with Southern California suntans very nearly explodes into gunplay. Out of a thicket of hard looks, swaggers, threats and homophobic insults emerges one fact: the snafu in the garage was not Redfoot's inspiration. Instead, it was engaged on the orders of a Mr Kobayashi (Pete Postlethwaite) – who now wants to meet the suspects. That promises still another, even starker confrontation but when it occurs, in a private pool-room, the suspects find themselves completely flummoxed by the appearance, demeanour and imperious demands of this strange figure. The scene ends with the suspects suddenly realising they are in thrall to Kobayashi's employer, the dreaded Keyser Soze.

As a result, in the third action scene, the shortest and the most stylised, the suspects once again revert from being free agents to taking on the role of rebelling against their masters. These new masters, Keyser Soze and his global criminal network, are not representatives of the law but act as if they constitute little less than a remorseless anti-law. Just before the action scene, we see one curiously truncated consequence of this ferocity when the suspects find the runaway Fenster's broken body at the mouth of a seaside cave and commence a hysterical argument about whether to bury him on the spot. This liminal moonlit image of these modern cavemen suddenly driven to the emotional and physical edge by ruthless barbarism is dramatically garbled. We don't for a moment believe that the irrepressible Fenster would ever cut and run. However, the spooked hunters now set out for the third time to trap three unsuspecting men. Once again the suspects are disguised, becoming electricians in overalls. They set the trap this time in the constricted space of an elevator in a

Split-second flash in the dark

Stylised violence

brand new skyscraper – which makes it the third transitional space dominated by a form of transport. Kobayashi and his two flunkeys enter the elevator and face forward. Hidden above the cubicle, the cheerful killer McManus is ready for action. As the elevator ascends the lights go out. In a gorgeously menacing shot, what looks like two momentary strokes of lightning briefly illuminate Kobayashi's impassive face. After a cutaway to the elevator shaft, the lights go up. The bodyguards are no longer visible. Singer frames the shot so that, recalling McManus's previous killings, two more smears of blood appear on the rear window of the elevator cubicle over the shoulders of the unflappable Kobayashi. Stylised repetition distances the violence.

At this point Singer and McQuarrie break the strikingly formal pattern they've set up for the three action scenes. The trap the suspects have set is successful: they trap their quarry, Kobayashi, alive. But, this time, that's not good enough. Their hunters' tactics are coolly outstripped by Kobayashi's mastery of strategy. On an unfinished floor of the new office building – a glossy paradigmatic site of the 90s booming economy – the suspects threaten Kobayashi. McManus, putting the pistol to his head, whispers insinuatingly in his ear. Baldwin ably captures the joy of sadism, but sometimes even a rock-solid commitment to violence won't do the trick. Kobayashi tells them what 'his employer' is prepared to do if they refuse to buckle under. To frame such ultimate threats within the vocabulary of labour relations, and within the spatial context of the office building, is disquieting. The first action sequence decisively delegitimised the police. This sequence paints at least a veneer of legitimacy over another system of coercion, which far exceeds the grasp of the police, Soze's nebulous but global network of profitable terror.

As if to demonstrate this, Kobayashi informs the frustrated team that Edie Finneran, Keaton's lawyer-lover, is upstairs, taking an extradition statement from an illegal immigrant – and that she will be horribly 'violated' before being murdered, if the usual suspects continue to resist the terms of Soze's offer of employment. The incredulous suspects, along with their triumphant captive, are seen grimly moving down another corridor. Through a glass partition, etched with Japanese script, all observe

The intimacy of verbal sadism

Globalisation etched in glass

Reflection as the distancing of affection

Edie at work, at a conference table, with a beefy bodyguard looming over her. With just a touch of relish, Kobayashi now spells out in precise and vicious detail how select relatives of each of the suspects will meet their doom if the suspects fail to cooperate. Point made, he joins Edie in the conference room. The bodyguard moves and the pained Keaton becomes visible as a reflection in the glass.

Kobayashi evidently has sufficient power to raise the exercise of violence to the level of an implacable discipline – far beyond the considerable resources of the suspects. Thanks to him, the suspects have already buried Fenster. (The loss of Fenster is truly a shame: Benicio del Toro's verbal dance of ineffability lifts his performance into quite another zone of looniness from either Baldwin's or Pollak's somewhat more predictable outings.) Kobayashi is untouchable and cannot be intimidated. The suspects' recourse to violence has hardly any impact on him, which may be why Singer chooses to stylise and abbreviate the show of violence, reducing it to two flashes of light and two smears of blood. Displaying no recognisable markers of criminality, Kobayashi's appearance within the sterile context of the office building intimates a convergence between the no-holds-barred rationales that govern both technocracy and the international criminality he represents. He looks like a businessman but he quietly delivers the most sinister lines in the whole film, due in no small measure to the almost uncanny stillness of Postlethwaite's performance. Such an assertion of the minor and often smudged distinction between business and crime goes back in film history at least as far as Sam Fuller's *Underworld U.S.A.* (1961). Here Singer updates this venerable association to the level of global capital in a shot that smoothly blends Japanese script, the probably Pakistani Kobayashi and the illegal immigrant Edie is interviewing. This allusion, with its compact array of power relations, demonstrates the effortless ascendancy of global capital over the paltry legalism of the nation-state. In any case, Mr Kobayashi's disguise (darkly complexioned third-world gentleman in a suit) is perfect: the beast within is nowhere to be seen. The suspects back down when threatened that Soze will set about attacking their relatives – which, as we know, is the exact threat that Soze met head-on by murdering his family. The devil with global reach is prepared to violate any human connection – which is the secret, Verbal tells us, of Soze's power.

When it opened in the United States in August 1995, *The Usual Suspects* was immediately and unsurprisingly bracketed with Tarantino's *Reservoir Dogs* – which, in turn, was compared to John Huston's *The Asphalt Jungle* and Stanley Kubrick's *The Killing* (1956). Both of these early 90s films directed by young men keenly aware of film history perform clever variations on the venerable genre of heist noir. For Singer, this parallel was an advantage. 'The strategy', he has said, 'was to regard it as a plus, not a minus – to make a film so different that after seeing it no one could even imagine comparing the story and the aesthetic, merely the set-up.'[15] Both films essentially begin in the violent aftermath of a big heist and then move both forward and backward in time, *Reservoir Dogs* unpredictably, *The Usual Suspects* relentlessly. By choosing to begin after the point of dramatic crisis, both films draw attention away from the main action. In *Reservoir Dogs*, the big heist scene – another jewel robbery – is so dispensable to the narrative that we never see it, even though it turns out to be a disaster. In dispensing with what one expects to be an absolutely obligatory scene, Tarantino concentrates on the frenzied interactions of characters severed from their original purpose. At least superficially more conservative, *The Usual Suspects* eventually delivers on its big shipboard assault scene. However, by the time the scene arrives, what actually takes place is immediately subject to qualification, questioning, interpretation and re-interpretation. One movie dismisses its central action while the other builds an elaborate architecture of mystery around it.

It's suggestive that these two films become searches for a traitor hidden in the midst of a group of professional criminals. With enormous appetite both films portray a particularly narrow model of masculinity, and its codes of behaviour, as if it formed an invariable and universally accepted standard. This model could be described as white guys who like to play with guns. As Harvey Keitel playing Mr Brown in *Reservoir Dogs* says, 'What you're supposed to do is act like a fuckin' professional.' Performance is inextricable from identity: the operative words are 'act like'. Tarantino, given his studied cultivation of an aesthetic of excess just barely kept in check by genre conventions, revels in this performative milieu, with its endless smart talk and smarter moves, to which he is often prepared to sacrifice both action and speed. Everybody remembers the excruciating torture scene. But the excess even of that scene might be best summed up in the decision to direct Michael Madsen's performance so that he is torturing his cop victim and dancing at the same time. Lacking even *The Usual Suspects*' single female role, *Reservoir Dogs* comically evokes the narrowness and rigidity of its coding of masculinity with the colour-coded naming scheme ascribed to its characters (Mr Pink, Mr White, Mr Brown and so on). This scheme has been rigidly applied by the old pro mastermind Joe specifically to prevent the criminals from knowing anything about each other – and that lack of knowledge is exactly what defeats them. Instead of the equality that helps the team of usual suspects to organise itself and gives their action scenes their feel of unpredictable exhilaration, the roles played by the multiple misters are assigned to them by the mastermind. *The Usual Suspects* demonstrates the potential endurance of the working team, until unexpectedly threatened by the sudden appearance of a hidden mastermind.

The misters are so keen on locating the 'fuckin' rat' that they sacrifice even their lives in the effort. Neither group of criminal professionals is equipped to see who that rat is. Or, what amounts to the same thing, the rat in both cases is too good a performer to be seen. In *Reservoir Dogs*, Tim Roth, playing the undercover cop who becomes Mr Orange, needs only to master a technique of authentic criminal storytelling to be accepted by the criminals. The glaring inability of the men in both films to isolate the traitor, or even to know that there is one, suggests that the constant necessity for the competitive performance of masculinity strips the ensemble of other resources. Or that if this masculinity is only a construction, a performance, then counterfeit performance is inevitable. In both films a character clings to his mistaken view of the identity of the 'fuckin' rat', the performer who is not a 'real' man in the context created until it's too late to recoup. This cruel self-betrayal afflicting both Mr Brown and Dave Kujan is the flip side of the obsessive desire to entrap other men that consumes the action of the hunting scenes. Both ends of this dynamic serve to keep the potential of a more responsive and expressive humanity trapped within the well-armoured male body.

Seizing upon the initial premise of the usual suspects, the film-makers reconstruct the possibilities of the solo act of male heroism or anti-heroism (choose your poison) – that is, of the representation of exceptional individual action – into a team concept. The five middling worker-bee crooks crack jokes in the lineup, submit belligerently to grilling and fester with growing resentment in the holding cell. All male, all white, all young, all apparently straight and uncommitted to anyone but themselves (with the partial exception of Keaton), they come to accept their common identity and then decide to realise what they have accepted, to act out the roles the cops have scripted for them. Each, Verbal tells us, has training in a specific area of criminal expertise. Alone, each can barely cut it; but multiply by five and you could get a geometric leap in criminal productivity.

The crooks of heist noir dream of one last big score, 'the killing' that will enable them to walk away from lives of crime. Imaginatively speaking, the big caper crystallises the forty or fifty years of all-but-unbearable law-abiding tedium common to most people's lives into ten or maybe twenty breathlessly illicit minutes. The caper, with its ever-

Kujan – over the line

present risks of sudden death and imprisonment, stands in as a compacted representation of the slow death and claustrophobic monotony of regular employment. The gang members, the personnel of the caper movie, are recruited by the boss mastermind on the basis of high-level job skills as safe-crackers, explosives experts or getaway men. The heist-planning sequence stylises what amounts to an on-the-job training session. Both *Reservoir Dogs* and *The Asphalt Jungle* feature such a scene, but *The Usual Suspects* avoids it. The disciplinary codes of corporate culture and the sometimes considerable problems involved in getting along with co-workers are reconfigured as the code of criminal culture and the lethal disagreements that often punctuate the heist film. Nevertheless, values of commitment, attention to detail and teamwork are common both to the workaday world and to the world of the caper movie. These inversions and values are visible in *The Usual Suspects* but they have been retrofitted for contemporary sensibilities. Take that impossible dream of what Hammett called 'The Big Knockover'. What's heroic about it is that it's a desperate all-or-nothing grab for freedom. That dynamic barely surfaces in *The Usual Suspects*. Only Keaton, the token romantic, early on expresses anything like that twisted desire to get out from under, to go straight or simply to get out that motivates a tormented array of characters like Dix Handley and Doc Riedenschneider in *The Asphalt Jungle* or Johnny Ingram and Dave Burke and Earl Slater in *Odds against Tomorrow* (Robert Wise, 1959).

While *The Usual Suspects* evinces affection for the self-enclosed milieu of the heist genre, it also discards key aspects of the standard narrative. Most obviously, the film's flashback structure forecloses the capacity of the present tense to build suspense, with the step-by-step build-up to the heist, the prolonged nerve-racking concentration on the robbery itself, up to the unpredictable moment when something goes terribly wrong during the robbery or the getaway, which leads inevitably to the team's dissolution, defeat, disaster. Instead, *The Usual Suspects* shifts narrative emphasis from the one big heist to what amounts to the team's six-week work history, culminating in the doomed assault on the boat. The concentration is shifted from the thing itself – the theft of property, the dramatic centre of heist noir – to what's left after it's over, after the team is broken up, the post-mortem. To accomplish this, the film adapts a confrontational scene that's nearly indispensable in crime narrative: the police station cop-on-criminal grilling. Furthermore, it stretches the dynamics of the confrontation to cover the entire story. According to Singer, 'The interrogation itself is almost a mirror for what the entire movie is about … In the interrogation, Kujan's professional agenda belies a lot about what he believes.'[16] With increasing intensity, the interrogation evokes something of the mode of the priest-on-sinner confessional in its attempt to identify the disguised source of evil, to get at the truth. And then, just as it refuses the ritualistic function of the lineup scene, the film blessedly manages to evade the all but religious moment in which the cop forces the crook to confess.

The most fully realised heist noir, John Huston's *The Asphalt Jungle*, was based on a novel by W. R. Burnett, a major hard-boiled writer (*Little Caesar*, *High Sierra*, *Nobody Lives Forever*). In his revision of Ben Maddow's script, Huston shifted its focus away from a stern police commissioner named Hardy who is bent on reforming a corrupt city.[17] Instead, initial shots catch big Dix Handley (Sterling Hayden) trudging through the seedy city streets just after dawn, dodging a prowl car, wind gusts slapping torn newspapers in its wake. It's all there: desperation, pursuit, the grip of time, alienation thick enough to cut with a knife, the refusal both to see things as they are and to give up without a fight. Soon, Handley is caught up in a scheme masterminded by Doc Riedenschneider (Sam Jaffe), an elaborate jewel robbery, bankrolled by a crooked lawyer. Almost everything that could go wrong does, but Doc's detailed plan nearly works despite this. Huston and Maddow catch each gang member at a sharpened point of vulnerability. Two of these small-time crooks already have jobs and everybody looks upon the heist more as just another job than a crime. Their idealisation of the task ahead of them, which soon crumbles, is framed by an authentically rendered milieu of crooked cops, hangers-on and bookie joints. Eventually, as much as a dozen different characters are given elbow room to play out specific contradictions between desire and mortality. As we have seen, McQuarrie's script deliberately sacrifices most of this psychological depth in favour of speed, action and violence, with only Keaton and Verbal Kint allotted much of this novelistic range.

Much of the first 'act' of *The Asphalt Jungle* dramatises how Doc recruits the criminal team. Each member's individual situation and affective relationships are sketched in some detail – and carefully differentiated. Strong motivations are provided for each character to accept the risks of the jewellery robbery – everything from simple greed ('money makes me sweat') to a costly operation for a sick wife to a lifelong itch to buy back the family farm. In *The Usual Suspects*, this introduction is abbreviated into montage sequences cut so tightly that you scarcely even catch the characters' names. In effect, *The Asphalt Jungle* develops five or six different if intertwining stories to capture the individual textures of its characters' lives. *The Usual Suspects*, in this respect less noir and more of a thriller, decisively sidesteps individual psychology.

The Asphalt Jungle and in their own way *The Killing* and *Odds against Tomorrow* show how uncontrollable, or at least unpredictable, frictions between character and situation conspire to prevent the heist's success. For example, Dix Handley's early outburst in *The Asphalt Jungle*, 'Don't bone me!' registers an all-too-touchy demand for respect that resonates throughout the film and means that he doesn't know when to quit. *Odds against Tomorrow* builds into a final, literally explosive blowout between the racist Earl Slater (Robert Ryan) and Johnny Ingram (Harry Belafonte), a black singer. *The Usual Suspects*, on the other hand, smoothly details how efficient the suspects are – at first. Their behaviour can seldom be faulted even during the climactic assault. They make few mistakes. They don't compromise the group. They register more as perfectly self-motivated workers, who set themselves a task, plan its execution and follow it through, than as character studies. They have no outside lives. All these elements – even, or especially, the amorality – mirror the concurrent dominant model of corporate teamwork, with its ideal of unreserved devotion to work licensing unlimited greed. In such work environments – whether it's the criminal milieu or corporate culture – personality can be extraneous.

McQuarrie has been forthcoming about the 'real-life' sources of his interest in the heist film. McQuarrie and Singer, along with their editor/composer, John Ottman, functioned as just such a goal-oriented team – best friends since boyhood who shared a dream and worked together unstintingly to produce this film. *The Usual Suspects* turned out to be one such Big Score. However, McQuarrie drew direct inspiration for his team of criminal workers from his own experience working as part of a team security force at a suburban New Jersey multiplex. The media later (following the success of the film) hyped this experience, elevating him to a detective. The amused McQuarrie says that 'The detective agency was a glorified security guard position. The biggest thing we did was security for this movie theater in Sawyerville, New Jersey.'[18] Ironically, the vibrant verbal byplay of the film's crooks is actually miming the everyday speech patterns of a bored team of young security guards.

McQuarrie describes the process by which he names his characters as if it took precedence over every other consideration, as if it created the condition in which he was able to write. And where do the names of the suspects and the other characters come from? They are nearly all inspired by the names of his co-workers in the legal firm in which he worked when he wrote the script. 'The name of the office manager of the law firm was Dave Kujan ... I was introduced ... to a lawyer at the firm and she said, This is Keyser Sume ... I began to pull names from other attorneys ...: Fred Fenster, a Jeff Rabin.'[19] In other words, the imaginary criminal team is literally an inverted transposition of a real legal team – in at least one dimension, mirror images of each other. 'I just was pulling ideas from my environment.' On the level of naming, the lineup of petty crooks is really a lineup of lawyers and legal aides. The submerged parallel this implies – between corporate and criminal teamwork – can be carried further than naming. The directness of McQuarrie's extravagant restaging of major elements of his own experience as a team player in the workaday world (how very close to the surface it is) is probably what gives such unusual vividness and resonance to the metaphor of the usual suspects. He wrote about the milieu from which he emerged in the idiom which could most comprehensively heighten both its contradictions and its effectiveness.

This seems an accurate if mischievous heightening of the popular perception that many lawyers are not much more than glorified crooks in suits.

Also lurking not very far under – in fact, shining through – the surface of the film is a contemporary portrait of how young men behave at work. The down-and-dirty duality of this rowdy criminal/security guard team anchors the complementary fantasy of a global master criminal who has secretly recruited the team for his own purposes. Luckily none of the actors cast as suspects were big stars (though Gabriel Byrne comes close – and Spacey quickly became a star, largely with this film as impetus). This also reinforced the underlying realism of McQuarrie's decision to detail the actions of the team rather than bothering to investigate individual psychology. The suspects exist not to live or to think or to feel, but to act – that is, to produce, while basking in the manly illusion that they are freely doing so, when in fact they are under strict compulsion. The unheroic suspects seem condemned to criminality in the way that in the 'real' world other such young workers seem channelled to non-criminality – or maintain a veneer of non-criminality as workers while at the same time engaged in a range of petty crime.

The film's target audience of young straight males raptly identified with this mirror image of nervy, violent, profane risk-takers who don't take shit from nobody nohow. The suspects have a plan and act on it. Young non-criminal workers must do what they're told, submitting to the master plan of the corporation that employs them, struggling all the while to retain a sense of justifiable resentment or justified security. McQuarrie's awareness of how such audiences react to criminal fantasies was immeasurably deepened by his own work experience at the Amboy multiplex. He has commented on his careful study of audience responses, honed in repeated daily showings of Hollywood films. The splashy simplicity of his character portraits is probably inspired by lessons learned during this workplace education in the consumption of entertainment.

McQuarrie's tactic of streamlining extends beyond his characters' psychologies. It also pertains to how he smoothes away ethical considerations. For instance, the suspects' Big Score, $91 million in *drug* money, is defined in advance as illicit and tainted. This helpfully codes the ill-fated shipboard heist as justifiable. Furthermore, Kobayashi not only blackmails them into the assault, he describes it in advance as suicidal. Similarly, the two smaller preparatory criminal schemes the suspects undertake more enthusiastically are morally coded in advance as not-really-hurting-anybody-who-doesn't-really-deserve-it-anyway. The first scam, the hijacking of New York's Finest Taxi Service, actually performs a public service by unmasking police corruption. Verbal's voiceover crows about the fifty-two cops who end up busted, thanks to the suspects' good deed. In effect, since the usual suspects are interested only in stealing from other criminals, they redefine crime as something that bad guys only do to other bad guys. Who but a bore or a stickler would think of such acts as actual theft?

The script's ethical hedges allow the suspects to register as inoffensively or interestingly criminal, properly uncomplicated and unambiguous objects of fantasy, who, it is true, might at worst be a mite trigger-happy. Such hedges are foreign to classic heist noir, which tends to be more straightforward. In *The Asphalt Jungle*, a jewellery robbery is a robbery – not a good deed. In *Odds against Tomorrow*, a bank robbery is a robbery. And so on. Crime in *The Asphalt Jungle* is referred to as 'a lefthanded form of human endeavour', but the crooks are all held accountable. A similar moral calculus pervades Kubrick's *The Killing* and Wise's *Odds against Tomorrow*.

McQuarrie's reductive excision of both psychological and moral conflicts among the suspects effectively streamlines the narrative to a series of violent confrontations with opposing teams: the cops who pick them up in the first place, the crooked cops who run New York's Finest Taxi Service, Redfoot's belligerent pack, the drug dealers ambushed in the parking lot, the thick-necked thugs protecting Kobayashi and finally the double team of Hungarian mobsters and Argentine sailors at the film's climax. In cleansing the narrative, McQuarrie is able to concentrate on the same attractions that have made professional team sports the primary passional pursuit of young men in the United States. What matters in each confrontation is sticking together, fearlessly acting out one's assigned role, and unalloyed aggression in the pursuit of winning. The usual suspects move with the precision of a SWAT team, even though there are no scenes in which they plan or coordinate their actions. The social order the film depicts abnegates the role of the individual (with the significant and conditioning exception of the evil mastermind). Instead, the script depicts a world ruled by brawling gangs out to steal each other's treasure.

3 On the Side of a Bus

I first encountered *The Usual Suspects* before its release in the form of a stark question plastered across a New York City bus: 'Who is Keyser Soze?' This ad campaign, as I remember, was clever enough to leave the film itself unnamed, slyly intimating that Keyser Soze, whoever he was, might even be a real person. The hook was in place. Janet Maslin, in *The New York Times*, dutifully granted the film 'cult status' the day it opened.[20] Generating repeat business among its target audience of young, white males, *The Usual Suspects* was highly successful at the box office – for a 'small', independently produced film. Critics generally praised McQuarrie's script for the same qualities that had caused Singer so much trouble with studios and producers when he was trying to finance the film: the density and speed of the plotting. Singer has said, 'I can't tell you all the companies that rejected it, just rejection, rejection.'[21] At one point, after getting European money, Singer had already opened offices and started casting when the deal fell through. His producer Robert Jones then set up a negative pickup deal with Polygram and Spelling – and they moved ahead quickly, especially since the actors were all taking cuts on their usual salaries. With the film bank-financed, Singer was happy: 'I got my deal and I also got a lot of freedom and power because the money was flowing from a bank as long as I stayed on schedule and on budget.'[22]

Singer came in under budget and on time for a thirty-five day shooting schedule in which all the locations were in New York City and San Pedro. The film earned $23.5 million on an investment of a little under $6 million. Its cachet was further enhanced when it won two Academy Awards, Best Original Screenplay and Best Supporting Actor (Kevin Spacey). However, its cultic aura probably emanates from its powerful evocation of remote-control evil and, more crucially, from the cleverness with which the ending confounds audience expectations – a puzzle that seemed to demand a second look to yield up its secrets. According to John Fried in *Cineaste*, since its release, the film 'has been immortalized on the Internet by hard-core fans devoted to … deciphering the film's elusive plot' and coming up with alternative answers to the question on the side of the bus.[23] Sadly, on the web even immortality turns out to be fleeting, as this frenzy has dwindled to a few intermittently maintained web fansites on the film and its director, and another handful devoted to the actors – particularly Spacey and, more recently, Benicio del Toro, since winning an Academy Award for his performance in *Traffic*.[24] A hint of the erstwhile web fervour persists on the Internet Movie Database site, where over 400 fans have written detailed evaluations of their favourite film. This same site's poll of the 250 greatest films ever made ranks *The Usual Suspects*, with over 45,000 votes, in fifteenth place. This elevation might seem surprising until you discover that the vast majority of these enthusiasts admit to being in the 18- to 29-year-old demographic. This confirms how well Singer and McQuarrie's youth has served them in capturing their cohort.

In any case, the invisible arch villain's name rapidly came into common usage as an ironic signifier for an unidentifiable agent of bad luck. This saw short-lived if everyday use as a joke – which involved a misreading of the film itself. If you walk away from the film wondering who Keyser Soze is, you've missed the point. Nevertheless, there was endless discussion about what really happened in it among general (i.e. young) audiences, in the same way that *Rashomon* (1950) and *Last Year in Marienbad* (1961) generated arguments in the heyday of the art movie. Perhaps not in the same way. Art-house audiences regularly hurled themselves into the quicksand of meaning. Pleasure-seeking multiplex audiences tend to stay on firmer ground.

Both the daily and weekly press were positive, sometimes explosively so. *San Francisco Examiner*: 'sensational'. *Los Angeles Times*: 'A maze you'll be happy to get lost in.' *Washington Post*: 'deliciously intricate'. *Newsweek*: 'The best, most stylish crime movie since Stephen Frears's 1990 *The Grifters*.'[25] And yet some writers also formed a kind of chorus of complaint: Roger Ebert said, 'I prefer to be amazed by motivation, not manipulation.'[26] 'A nasty shaggy dog story,' said Georgia Brown in *The Village Voice*, 'in which nothing made sense or mattered.'[27] It's interesting that even critics and reviewers filled with enthusiasm like Anthony Lane in

The New Yorker said: 'I still haven't figured out exactly what happens.'[28] The slightly submerged terms of this dual response seem to indicate that it's the very same aspect of the film to which both pro and con responded so strongly.

In the long run the film has received little sustained criticism. Instead, it occupies a critical highwater mark that sets the trickiness standard. For example, a *New York Times* review of Christopher Nolan's *Memento* (2000) rhapsodises that it's 'a brilliant feat of rug-pulling, sure to delight fans of movies like *The Usual Suspects*'.[29] In this way a sort of disparagement has been endorsed. *The Usual Suspects* appears to trick its viewers rather than really engaging them. In her otherwise enthusiastic review, Janet Maslin complained that the film never touches 'one important base: the audience's emotions. This movie finally isn't anything more than an intricate feat of gamesmanship.'[30] Christopher Tookey in *The Daily Mail* admits that 'the film draws you into the amoral mind-set of professional criminals as cleverly as any picture since *The Asphalt Jungle*.' But then he complains that

its main appeal is as a puzzle picture, a small, intellectual sub-section of the thriller genre. It is too cerebral to succeed with mainstream audiences and, unlike that other over-complicated thriller, *The Big Sleep*, fails to make us care enough about the characters to tolerate the rococo intricacies of its plot.[31]

His claim that the ending 'will leave many people feeling cheated and dissatisfied' is echoed by Foster Hirsch, who gives short shrift to the film in his book *Detours and Lost Highways: A Map of Neo-Noir*: 'Crime here really has, and is of, no consequence; what counts is story construction, how the filmmakers built their clever noir puzzle.'[32]

This divided reaction often afflicts movies with surprise endings. A voiceover from out of nowhere at the end of *Witness for the Prosecution* (1957) pleads with audiences not to reveal its rather absurd trick ending. Similarly, during the initial release of Hitchcock's *Psycho* (1960), audiences were urged not to reveal its plot twists. For many years *Psycho* was automatically regarded as a less 'serious' Hitchcock film, a mere shocker. The ending of *The Usual Suspects* is obviously intended to be surprising and unsettling. Reviewers respected the convention of not revealing the surprise in their reviews, but opinions varied on the question of manipulation. For some it was a breach of contract with the audience, for others a thrilling sleight of hand. The *Washington Post*: 'After following the beckoning twists and turns you're left trapped and more than a little disappointed.'[33] The *New Yorker*'s Anthony Lane: 'McQuarrie's script stays one step ahead of us, or so we believe; in the closing minutes, it becomes clear that we have in fact been trailing ten miles behind. The more movies one watches, the easier it is to spot the planting of a twist; the joy of being outsmarted, therefore, grows more precious by the year.'[34]

In effect, adverse critics were charging the film-makers with little less than aesthetic fraud. It seemed a little too much that the narrator's flashbacks were revealed to be unreliable only in the very last moments. Since these flashbacks made up the meat of the film, it became impossible to tell the difference between what had really happened and what the narrator had made up. If a film-maker wanted to get away with a scam like that he ought to be making an art movie, not a mere thriller.

It was all right, in fact it was fine, for Kurosawa's intensely emotional and refined *Rashomon* to tell its tragic story with a complex, almost musical, arrangement of conflicting flashbacks from the points of view of different characters. Viewers realised early on that there might not be one 'true' whole story. This discovery made it possible and even exciting to participate in the film's evocation of the fragility of subjectivity, the relations between desire and violence and to wonder how those issues related to the necessary partiality of storytelling. And it was clear from its first stylish moments that there wasn't much literal sense to be made of the narrative of *Last Year in Marienbad* even if you sweated over it. But to get a tough, complicated plot rolling in an action movie and then to weasel out of it by unmasking the narrator as a conman at the very last moment – wasn't that breaking one of the primary laws of mainstream narrative movies? The sticking point is how kosher it is to change the rules of the

game when the game's almost over. What if the film has been constructed
to put the problem of fidelity to a code, of conforming to the rules of
perception, to the test? What if the film-makers wanted to implicate the
audience in the consequences of that fidelity?

Singer has said that he was primarily interested in portraying the
implications of misplaced perception: 'Perception, the difference between
what you believe and what really is, is the central theme.'[35] However, the
film-makers almost invariably think through and visualise the perceptual
deceptions necessary to mystery narrative in terms specific to male
identity. For instance, early on, before Verbal's first flashback in the San
Pedro police station, Kujan hands him a lighter. Try as he might, Verbal
can't get the lighter open with his good right hand. Finally, Kujan lights his

Subtly feminised

Technology is too late

cigarette. McQuarrie says that Singer added this compelling bit of business on set.[36] The act subtly feminises Verbal and physically encapsulates the apparent balance of power between the two men. In the film's first scene, the unidentifiable Keyser Soze, using only his left hand, effortlessly lights a cigarette before murdering Keaton. Those contrasted images – a physically adept and a physically inadequate man both using lighters – block us from imagining that the two men could actually be one and the same. This narrative manipulation (or deception) is underwritten by the fact that the style in which a man lights a cigarette is coded to excess as a key performance of masculinity in film.

At the same time, for most audiences and many critics the unreliable narrator, played with fully imagined detail by Kevin Spacey, was key to the film's most intense pleasure: the moment when the 'weakest' character is revealed to be the 'strongest'. As he walks out of the police station, the gimp Verbal Kint, having been forced by his adversary, Dave Kujan, to tell the story of the brief rise and sudden fall of the usual suspects, becomes the mastermind personification of evil, Keyser Soze. (Verbal's lame leg, we now realise, is the mundane equivalent to Satan's cloven hoof; his widow's peak Satan's customary coiffure. Singer attributes this 'geeky' haircut to Spacey's inspiration.[37]) Left behind – as a sketch of the evil one's face emerges from the fax machine just a moment too late – is the audio recording of the story he'd deliberately hobbled with who knew how many lies and inventions. Technology is either too little or too late to fulfil its supposedly objective role in assessing guilt.

The contest between the two men, the criminal and the cop, had not in the end been about the truth of the story. Ira Nayman points out that 'a conversation between two police officers confirms' what Verbal has told the police about the first heist. 'This objective corroboration … validates it for the audience.'[38] The script cannily salts the unreliable narration with early moments of reliability. In the end, we never discover the exact truth but we do find out which of the two men controlled access to that truth. We do see who wins the power struggle. Verbal's escape destabilises the police control of the narrative. Out on the street, Verbal's perverse transformation from cripple to commander embodies his creative twisting of truth and falsehood. His palsied body regains its true shape in the dark triumph of illegitimacy. Sitting in the darkened multiplex, the audience takes illicit pleasure in Verbal's escape from the machine of the law.

Who is Verbal – up to the fatal moment when he betrays us by becoming someone else?

He is introduced not as a narrator, but as a sworn witness. Speaking from a position literally before the law, he first becomes visible sitting spotlighted in front of the official seal of the great state of California. The framing, the encircling seal and the lighting all reinforce the centrality of

Weakest or strongest?

Introduced as a sworn witness

this witness. As the only survivor of the suspects, he alone is in a position to tell the story.

However, this visual centrality is deliberately deceptive. Verbal is actually an unusually marginal narrator who never tires of emphasising how marginal he is – it was a 'lucky accident' that he even got to be one of the usual suspects, he says. Meek and meagre and physically handicapped, Verbal is at the very least a marked contrast to the voiceover narrators of classic noir. These tough guys are usually played by burly leading men unlike the comparatively slight and slyly tentative Kevin Spacey. Rather than actually being notorious, Verbal happily says, 'I got to feel notorious', virtually admitting that he is playing a role. The classic noir narrator also speaks a tersely vivid vernacular that emerges from the hard-boiled novel, an arena in which Verbal's ingratiating conman's patter would be despised. As soon as he sits down to be interrogated by Kujan, Verbal begins bubbling over with irrelevant autobiographical anecdotes: 'Tension is a killer. I used to be in a barbershop quartet in Skokie, Illinois – the baritone was this guy named Kip Diskin. Big fat guy. I mean like Orca fat. He used to get so stressed in the—.' For one critic, Stanley Orr, Verbal's excessive production of such details 'bares the constructive machinery by which a reality is generated' with all the deceptive purity interrogated by Roland Barthes in his consideration of how fiction manages to create a reality effect.[39] The very insignificance of such detail serves to authenticate

Verbal tease: 'one time my piss came out like snot'

Verbal's testimony. Verbal is nervous and often sycophantic while under police questioning, but he is also a conman with an agenda. Knowing that he will be released within two hours, he tries to fill up the time with jabber. In the end, Verbal turns out to be far more in control than his excessive verbalism would lead us to expect. McQuarrie has pointed out that although in his script 'Verbal's presented as a dummy', the more Singer and Spacey developed the character the smarter he got. McQuarrie's comment that 'you're so busy trying to figure out what he knows, you don't stop to think who he is' hints at the degree to which knowledge overtakes value in experiencing the film.[40]

The prospect of impending freedom gives Verbal a different stature and function than his apparent forebears in films like *Out of the Past* (1947), *D.O.A.* (1950), *Double Indemnity* (1944) and *The Postman Always Rings Twice* (1946). For these narrators, speaking at or near the moment of death, when the story ends so does life. The narrator of *The Usual Suspects* walks out of the San Pedro police station and out of the film. For classic noir narrators, storytelling is an unburdening that can, perhaps, lead to redemption. But there's nothing redemptive about Verbal's story: it's strained and edgy and it eventually breaks down completely. As he tearfully leaves the office just before the end of the film, his story doesn't seem coherent any more. Under the pressure and physical intimidation of his interrogator, he seems no longer sure what happened on board the

The climax of Verbal's act

Argentine boat. Reluctantly, he gives way to Kujan's version. The
redemption the classic noir narrators seek is clearly dependent on closure.
They must bring their story to a satisfying form of completion which
usually encompasses their own mortality. Verbal fails this test as well. He
stands just outside the doorway of the office and mutters, 'fuckin' cops',
and then limps away. Thus, even before the next decisive twist, the long
moment of identification, Verbal has undermined the classic flashback
narrator.

The noir narrator nearly always characterises himself as a man drawn
into a criminal world almost against his will. Verbal is already a small-time
conman when the story begins. Consider the narrator of *D.O.A.*, Frank
Bigelow (Edmond O'Brien), an ordinary certified public accountant,
accidentally caught in the grip of corruption. He journeys away from
home, away from domesticity, to the big city and, taking yet another risk,
goes to a party with strangers and is poisoned by radioactive iridium. The
uniqueness of the film lies in its unrelenting focus on the fact that Bigelow
is a dying murder victim who takes on the role of his own detective. Given
his desperation, his race against time, Bigelow often addresses his
flashbacks to the sceptical police in hostile or demanding tones. Verbal, in
contrast, appears to be only a witness-participant, a team-player, who
wants out. Verbal is always manoeuvring around the ever-tightening
machine of the plot as he plays out his role with Kujan. Emphasising his
desire to cooperate with the police, he scarcely ever raises his voice. He
knows that it pays to be agreeable. And, as a conman, he can use his
apparent weakness to placate and disarm his threatening antagonist.
Bigelow must tell the whole story truly to attain his redemption. Verbal
must tell the story well enough to make it seem whole and true. Intimacy
and vulnerability stand in for veracity. To survive, one must create and
maintain at all costs a publicly credible fiction about oneself. This
requirement is foreign to the essentially romantic noir narrator –
condemned to tell the awful truth, a truth that both voiceover and visuals
verify. Or, as Frank Krutnick puts it, 'What is especially remarkable about
D.O.A. is the figuration … of the narrative itself as an instrument of
grotesquely exaggerated (self-)persecution.'[41]

The aggression and fatalism of the noir hero are alien to Verbal. He is protected. The DA, the mayor and the governor, we are told very early on, have all insisted on his release. This triple-whammy political pressure nearly prevents Kujan from being able to question him – and serves to verify the corruption of the justice system at every level. Corruption is endemic to noir, but the narrator is usually its target not its beneficiary. Not only is Verbal not trapped, he has mysteriously been given immunity from prosecution, a measure of Keyser Soze's invisibly satanic influence in the corridors of power.

Furthermore, the typical male noir narrator is all too ripe for devouring by the classic noir *femme fatale*. This motif is absent in *The Usual Suspects*. Like three of the other four suspects, Verbal is not only sexually unattached, at first he projects the quietly efficient nun-like asexuality of someone long convinced that he's not even a player. However, in three early flashback scenes alone with Keaton, Verbal takes on the role of slowly detaching the dark Irishman from his relationship with the only female character, his lawyer-lover-business partner, Edie Finneran. During these scenes, Verbal uses his unspoken envy of everything he knows he will never have to manipulate Keaton – with enough emotional complexity that he increases our sympathy for him. In the end, Spacey's performance is ambiguous enough to suggest that Verbal is infatuated with Keaton. When Kujan tries to browbeat Verbal into

Affection or infatuation?

identifying Keaton as Keyser Soze, he is met with Verbal's openly emotional, stirringly abject outburst, 'He was my friend!'

Verbal cunningly asserts his array of differences during the police station scenes. He manages to appear as marginal, feminised, emotional – exhibiting everything but tough-guy behaviour. While this appears to be no more than another performance – difference as masquerade – in the process he completely disarms the law, delegitimising the force of the law without resorting to violence. His performance of weakness enacts a viable if only tactical critique of the masculine character that struts through the rest of the film. In the end, as Verbal disappears Soze appears, silently rather than verbally demonstrating the instability of masculine identity by proving that the weakest of men could also be the strongest.

However, crucial as it is, it's not only the carefully constructed instability of the narrator that puts the construction of masculinity into question in the course of the film.

During the scene in the holding cell, the distinctive undercurrent of the connection that the five suspects begin to make is a kind of self-conscious, aggressively profane, homophobic and strictly verbal homoeroticism common among young white dudes who think of themselves as straight. Here and elsewhere, the suspects frequently address each other as 'ladies'. Few scenes pass without shuttling between threats of violence and taunting suggestions of repressed desire, as if the two were interchangeable. When a cop threatens suspect Todd Hockney with a jail term, he offers to 'fuck your father in the shower, then have a snack'. In the holding cell, when Fenster mutters about the cops having a 'finger up my asshole', Hockney jokes, 'Oh, I didn't know it was Friday', and Fenster asks him, 'Do you want some?' Solemnly offering a voiceover tribute to the suspects' toughness, Verbal concludes with his most sincere compliment: 'These guys would never bend over for anybody.' McQuarrie says he borrowed this talk from his co-workers in the security force. The free-floating homosexual raillery adds a dimension of desire, a homosocial intensity, to the team. As Singer recalls, 'There was a very homoerotic sense of humour on the set. I think that's essential – ever since those guys got together to kill Julius Caesar. Bunch of guys in a bath house talking about killing.'[42]

The script allows no one but Keaton a visible heterosexual attachment. Even this is associated not with sexual desire but with the desire for legitimacy, with girlfriend Edie described by McManus as Keaton's 'meal ticket'. And it's true that their professional relationship is also emphasised. The first time we see them in the restaurant where the cops pick him up, they're trying to swing a deal with potential investors. They have exactly one scene alone together outside the New York police station. First Edie talks about filing suit against the cops. Then she's eager to tell him she loves him – but he scarcely notices, since he's obsessing about how his chances to open a restaurant must now be in ruins. The potential intimacy of this scene is blocked in other ways. Like the lineup, it's shot to resemble a kind of performance. This time the emphasis is not on the performers but on the audience. While Keaton and Edie talk, their bodies are theatrically framed by the entrance to the station house. The other suspects, whom you might think would be anxious to get away quickly after many wasted hours, instead stand conspicuously across the street to watch the couple. Why? Keaton has refused their offer to join in their first caper, a hijacking. Ostensibly, they may be hanging out in the hope that he'll dump the dame and get with the programme. But a series of three eyeline match-cuts between Keaton and the other suspects hammer that home. Spread out on the dark street staring at Keaton, the young men look like they're cruising. And he looks interested.

Richard Dyer has argued that classic noir manifests 'a certain anxiety over the existence and definition of masculinity and normality'.[43] And, as James Naremore points out in *More Than Night: Film Noir in Its Contexts*, most of the same films depend on a fierce displacement of the patriarchal family, the site from which the presumably determining conditions of the construction of masculinity emerge.[44] Not content with mere displacement, *The Usual Suspects* banishes the family with almost unprecedented violence in favour of the social grouping of the young, all-male team.

The severity of the film's repression of sexuality – except as noted in the suspects' strained banter – is remarkable (though not exceptional:

Are they cruising?

Is he interested?

Reservoir Dogs is similar). Heist films are almost by definition intense depictions of men involved in a criminalised work process. In a sense, the heist film both redeems and represses the labour process by representing it as an all-or-nothing one-time venture. Nevertheless, in the history of the genre these teams of worker-crooks are very rarely men without women. The heat, the longing, the desperation for another kind of life that courses through the genre demands the accompaniment of such performances. Marie Windsor's greedy, two-timing Sherry in *The Killing*. Gloria Grahame's perverse Helen in *Odds against Tomorrow*, who gets sexually

Keeping the only woman at a distance

excited when the half-demented racist Earl tells her what it felt like to kill a man. Jean Hagen's grateful Doll Conovan in *The Asphalt Jungle*, who falls for the hooligan Dix mainly because he's one of the few men who haven't abused her.

The striking absence of women from *The Usual Suspects* is due in part to dramatic economy, to a deliberate intention to forego the pauses of emotional involvements in favour of the speed of action. This is evident in the considerably streamlined treatment of the Keaton/Edie relationship, some of which was cut from McQuarrie's original script. For instance, in the script, when Verbal shows up at her apartment to convince Keaton to take part in the Taxi Service heist, Edie is present to argue with Verbal and dramatise her support of Keaton.[45] McQuarrie approves of such cuts: 'We liked the idea that Edie was, as the story developed, less of a character and more of a representation of Keaton's other life. In the film, there's always glass, or some other barrier, between them.'[46] But such a choice has other implications. The excision of attachments helps to model a world in which ruthlessness is not merely an attitude but a value, a world in which everything extraneous (including women) can be and should be distanced and then repressed in favour of the common goal. (As Verbal says of Keyser's decision to wipe out his own family: 'One cannot be betrayed if one has no people.') Of course, the suspects' almost automatic association of sexuality with violence inevitably suggests a fear of sexuality that in classic noir was personified by the *femme fatale*. That drastically overworked figure is absent in *Suspects*, but the fear has become generalised. To the extent that women are represented at all, they become unfortunate impediments to the absolute exercise of male will and ambition.

But so, by extension, are all the other sensual pleasures of life. Except for a perfunctory few moments when the suspects play pool (immediately interrupted by the sudden appearance of the sinister Mr Kobayashi, who in placing his briefcase on the pool table puts a stop to that), we never, throughout the course of the film, see them participating in any pleasurable everyday activity, except smoking. In fact, we never see them except when they are in the midst of working or planning to work.

And, remarkably enough, they never even express a vagrant desire for another life. They reap an extraordinary profit from their first heist, but no one indulges himself – even for a moment. It's on to the next gig. The workaholic crook might count as a new category in criminology. Coincidentally or not, this profile fits the drastic extension of the working day typical of one kind of ambitious white-collar worker in the buzzing American economy of the 80s and 90s, in which nothing mattered except making your bundle and where conspicuous consumption seemed less about pleasure than staging and justifying the drive to keep working and earning and winning.

The film dramatises the dire consequences of the powerless usual suspects' attempt prompted by the initial spur of revenge, to take power through teamwork. But, since their imagination goes no further than that, they condemn themselves to run their initial impulse toward some kind of freedom into the ground, i.e. to repeat themselves. Verbal even comments in a voiceover, at the point when Keaton is about to stall once again before undertaking the second heist, that 'a man can't change what he is'. As if endorsing this notably anti-dramatic concept of character, the film-makers concentrate unswervingly on masculinity as no more and no less than the performance of power. The suspects are thus vulnerable to a more ruthless enactment of this principle – in this case, one founded on the refusal of the most basic human connections (the family). Every contact between the male characters betrays the volatility of the relations between some projection of masculine desire (not usually sexual) and the assertion of power or control. Being a man is modelled as a test every character must take over and over again. Passing the test is at best a provisional success, a temporary affirmation; failing it gets you killed.

Verbal's flashbacks to the suspects' exploits are all shot with relatively straightforward objectivity, with the exception of the flashback to Keyser Soze's murder of his family. But that appears, first time round, to be additional business, part of the background. For the rest, there are straight cuts to the past and back again to the present. There is no attempt at stylisation – no dissolves, wipes or soft-focus transitions as visual correlatives to the strange workings of memory. A lot of visual clutter is thereby avoided – full speed ahead.

In any case, the flashback to the suspects' reluctant assault on the Argentine boat in San Pedro harbour – a long, complicated scene which ate up six days of a thirty-five day shoot – is easily the most densely edited sequence in the film. It's interrupted at one point by a short scene that returns to Verbal and Kujan in the police station. The suspects have been assigned to find and destroy an object – a $91 million mountain of cocaine – that's nowhere in sight (another absence in a film rife with them). Soze's number one man, Mr Kobayashi, has blackmailed the suspects into undertaking this suicidal attack while misleading them about its object, which is not cocaine but a heretofore unseen foreign gentleman stuck in a brig below decks, who is able to identify Soze and is about to be traded to the dreaded Hungarian mobsters for a truck full of money. The suspects are unaware that they have really been sent to clear the ground while Soze manages to board the boat and assassinate his enemy.

Early in this scene, Keaton persuades Verbal to sit out the engagement. We can guess that he intends to bring their friendship to some resolution – though Keaton says he wants Verbal to stay alive in order to tell Edie what happened. It seems notably illogical to reduce the team to a group of three, except that Singer and McQuarrie have structured all the previous action scenes around the rule of three victims. This time out they are pretty sure they will become the victims. However, they manage to launch the attack successfully. The obstreperous McManus is stuck uttering lines like 'Elvis has left the building' and, after managing to get six or eight Hungarians in the sights of his rifle, 'Oswald was a fag.' After shooting all the foreigners in sight, Keaton and McManus go below in search of the white mountain, a sequence that is full of many menacing point-of-view shots. Meanwhile, Hockney commandeers the van chock full of cash. Suddenly, an invisible assailant kills Hockney. Blood splashes onto the cash. McManus and Keaton eventually tire of waving their weapons around. In a fury, Keaton realises that the cocaine is no more than a mirage. Back up on deck, Keaton is shot from behind. Emerging from a dark hatchway, McManus pitches forward with a very serious knife sticking out of the back of his neck. I must admit I was sorry to see this knife. McManus has been far too ferocious and jocular a killer to be done in so effortlessly. His accomplishments have earned him a more compelling send-off than Singer allows him.

The pattern of the earlier action scenes remains visible: three men done in by an unexpected attack at a transitional site, involving a vehicle – only this time the suspects are the victims of the hunt. We guess that their unseen assailant must be Soze. But there's something unsettling about this cluster-killing. Soze's sudden proximity (even if still off-screen), instead of heightening seems to short-circuit the visual impact of these crucial slayings. It's tough to find effective solutions to the problem of depicting three variations on a murder if the actor must remain off-screen. Singer

The miracle of death

Not the most imaginative send-off

knew how to stage the previous action scenes as contests, with the combatants in view. When the suspects become mere employees, they seem to lose not only their lives but their muscular heroism. What has been compelling about them is their amoral lunge for autonomy – their refusal to knuckle under.

Then the film comes full circle, returning to where it started ('last night'), with Keaton paralysed and wasted on the deck, and everyone else, except for the still unrecognisable Soze, apparently dead. Soon after a cutaway to Verbal looking anxious, we see the foreign gentleman obligingly looking very scared and begging for mercy. The off-screen Soze murders him as well.

The following, even more densely edited scene, recovers the theme of male contestation, displacing it to the police station, and depicts the final struggle between Verbal and Kujan. Kujan maintains that Keaton must be Soze – as if he was able to flashback to what he has never seen, or could force Verbal to re-imagine events that didn't happen. (Gabriel Byrne also claimed to be confused about who Soze was: 'During shooting and until watching the film, I thought I was.') We see Keaton as Soze executing someone on the deck of the boat, an act we are in a position to know never occurred. We see that Kujan's imagination has been warped by his hatred of Keaton. Kujan insists that Verbal didn't really watch Soze shoot Keaton. Technically, he's correct. Verbal claims Keaton as his friend despite Kujan's jeers. You were useful to Keaton, Kujan says, because you were weak and stupid and a cripple. While both Verbal and Kujan passionately marshal false arguments and misinformation about their chosen but unavailable object of desire and hatred, the Keaton who was not Soze, our sympathy flows toward the conscious misinterpreter. Using that often decisive psychological weapon of the weak, vulnerability, Verbal appears to give way. A little later we realise how expert he is at feinting. And Kujan, we now become certain, has never been fighting for the truth of what happened. He's always had an axe to grind. Verbal creates a malleable fiction that guarantees him an out, while Kujan turns out to be trapped by his fixed ideas.

In noir, the big heist scene (and/or its aftermath, the getaway) is always suicidal. Something goes wrong that the planning hadn't foreseen.

Kujan tries to get at the truth

The team of crooks are supposed to be twisted dreamers, if not just plain twisted. The usual suspects never do learn how to dream. They are even denied the drab but moving grace allotted to Dix Handley in *The Asphalt Jungle*, who breathes his last amid the grasses of his dispossessed pappy's Kentucky field alongside a sovereignly indifferent horse. Singer and McQuarrie dispose of the suspects hastily, with a touch of embarrassment, once this autonomous team of troublemakers allow themselves to be reduced to the status of mere employees, a fate equivalent to death. To the degree that these ordinary criminal workers lived out the principle of autonomous movement, they'd offered a fleeting image of the possibility that resistance might crop up where you least expected it.

4 The Shattered Coffee-cup

In both film and literature, the crime narrative, more thoroughly than other kinds of storytelling, lays claim to a goal of transparency. What this means is that in the crime story we expect even the most mysterious events to yield at the end to a complete explanation. The figure of the detective as rational seeker of the linear truth, as master explainer, is the usual guarantor of this claim to clarity. *The Usual Suspects* frustrates, upsets and then denies this claim. After constructing what seems like a credible story, certain facts, major or minor, are withheld and therefore the story can never be reassembled into its complete and completely satisfying linear form. This form of retelling is obligatory in the final scene of the crime/detective narrative (even more obligatory than the confrontation between victim and criminal in the lineup scene). At that point, all the loose ends are tidied up. The murderer is named by the superior figure of the rational all-knowing detective in the course of retelling the story of the murder itself. The mystery is dispelled, and, most crucially and coincidentally, order is restored, the social fabric is remade, state morality reasserted.

In *The Usual Suspects*, Kujan struggles mightily but unsuccessfully for an explanation of what really happened to the usual suspects. In the end, he is left standing in the street as Soze is driven away from the police station by his lieutenant Kobayashi. Singer shoots the bewildered Kujan in broad daylight as everyday life surges chaotically around him. No restoration of order is possible. The detective cannot use storytelling to rationalise events. He has been defeated: the rationality presumed to ground the legal system has been put in doubt. Singer chose to enhance this effect even further with a last-minute decision during production to put Kobayashi into the scene. By this point we are inclined to believe that Verbal had made up this screwy character in the course of his narrative. But, as Singer says of the nature of the game, 'If you put one grain of truth in a story it makes the whole lie believable.'[47]

With Soze's escape, the spectre of violence, murder and chaos continues to pervade, if not to dominate – and on a scale the film describes as global. Such a view is hardly reassuring but it may be accurate

– which is to say, ultimately and ironically, it represents a more rational view of how the world works. Or, one might take the position that the ground of ultimate knowledge in relation to the forces of order and good has been ceded in the film to the ground of ultimate knowledge in relation to the forces of disorder and evil – a sleight of hand that may involve an equally drastic simplification. What is more certain is that the criminal in this case is no ordinary murderer. Nor is he that other Prince of Darkness popularised in 90s crime narratives, the serial murderer. He is depicted as the kaiser of the global criminal economy.

At the moment when Kujan is beginning to realise he's been had, a suspense-laden music cue gives way to a voiceover reprise of Kujan's words at the beginning of his film-length encounter with Verbal: 'Convince me.' Kujan turns out to have been spiked by his own words: Verbal did convince him. To convince someone, you certainly don't have to bother with the truth. All you have to do is to make a show of believing the story you're telling. We're told early on that Verbal's an experienced conman but see no evidence of his skill. Of course, if a conman is any good, we aren't going to realise it. In order for Singer to make the con apparent he has to loosen Verbal's stranglehold on the narrative. He finally gets Verbal out of that windowless confessional box of an office. He lets the narrative relax just a bit, leaving Kujan sitting bemusedly on the edge of the desk, idly staring at the bulletin board.

At this moment, when the story feels like it's over, since the storyteller has at last exited the scene, Singer approaches the answer to the film's central enigma. The answer comes from three directions at once, in three distinct forms: as a fairly primitive drawing emerging unnoticed out of a fax machine in the San Pedro police station; as a stunned, belated realisation signified by the shattering of a coffee-cup dropped by Kujan; and finally by the physical transformation of Verbal Kint into Keyser Soze. Once again, the rule of three.

The fragile everyday object, the coffee-cup, is shattered three times over in slow motion, a stylised repetition that signifies the shattering of the credibility of Verbal's narrative, the shattering of our complacent acceptance of the narrative and the realisation that the pieces are too numerous and too disparate ever to be glued back together. Singer provides an extreme close-up on one fragment. The words 'Kobayashi' and 'porcelain' and 'Indonesia' become visible to us (though not to Kujan). 'Kobayashi' becomes a floating signifier as we realise that the Japanese-ness that seemed to apply somehow to Soze's prime employee was no more than Verbal's serendipitous invention on the spot.

Verbal's escape from the police station impacts, by contrast, as a comic surprise. The escape is itself rapidly intercut with the detective's dawning awareness that he's been played for a fool: he rushes off in a futile attempt to detain his rapidly departing nemesis. The details of this editing sequence, which takes the audience into the joke, emphasise Kint/Soze's cleverness, so that the audience may not feel that it's being made fun of. The dumb cop is the butt. Suddenly the Verbal who has soaked up every ounce of available audience identification straightens out his crippled body. A tracking shot shows us Verbal's slow crippled walk becoming a vigorous stride.

The physical transformation unites radically contradictory performances of masculinity: hidden under the cover of Kint's abject, locally manipulative masochism is Soze's imperiously controlling, globally manipulative sadism. This dynamic of disguise connects to both sides of the originating John List story. Verbal's persona evokes List, the pathetic

The pieces begin to come together

The coffee-cup shatters

accountant whom no one could have imagined was capable of doing what Soze did to his family. Verbal completely occludes the other List – the mass murderer who hid for eighteen years under a pseudonym. In the same way, the international criminal mastermind wears the disguise of a gimp.

The film is concerned to depict Soze's criminality as relentlessly brutal and multinational. Singer and McQuarrie *globalise* the theme of invisible domination that shadows and mocks the visible domination of the law. The film is replete with references, characters and plot elements from several continents. French is spoken early in the film by two investors consulting with Keaton as the police swoop in. Keyser Soze may

From gimp to evil genius

be Turkish with a German father, but Hungarian mobsters are after him, and the ship the usual suspects attack in San Pedro is from Argentina. And, to rub it in, Mr Kobayashi, despite his Japanese-sounding name, is played by Postlethwaite, an English actor, with the complexion, manners and accent of an educated gentleman from Pakistan. And then there's Redfoot, the tall blond fence falsely bearing the name of a Native American, which is really the alias of an African-American woman. Soze, according to Kobayashi, believes that the suspects are all in debt to him because they have in various ways all interfered with his gun-running to Ireland or an illegal shipment to Pakistan – a range of activities that gives him the unconscionable reach of a multinational corporation. It's tempting to read such globalised domination as a barely disguised ultra-malevolent figure for that other force increasingly seen as demonic in its ruthless demand for profit at the expense of all other values, the multinational capitalism which pitilessly rules the world's economies without opposition in the post-communist era. In which case, Keyser Soze becomes a brand name.

It's hard to imagine any other actor of his generation as primed as Spacey to maintain such a subterranean aspect to his character for the length of an entire film. The colossal arrogance of his role as the producer in *Swimming with Sharks* (George Huang 1994) is inverted. Here his keynote is an equally colossal meekness. In playing a minor-league conman, Spacey is careful always to exploit the pathos of the odd man out – but to exploit it precisely by not calling undue attention to it. He projects the impression that he'd like to be one of the guys, but he's not so deluded as to think he ever really could be. He makes no special claims because of his affliction – he only refers to it in passing as 'CP', touchingly unaware, it seems, that not everybody stows that abbreviation in their mental dictionary. Through his basset-eyed refusal to take power during the interrogation scenes that frame and introduce the flashbacks, he gradually accumulates the film's entire emotional weight. His foil, Chazz Palminteri as Kujan, invariably comes on strong in an effort to fill up all the spaces Spacey opens up. Spacey makes it entertainingly impossible to tell when Verbal's loquacity is

sheer pleasure in hearing his own voice, or purposeful obfuscation to keep
the cops off-balance, or obliviousness to other people's interests. Playing
with a range of possibilities, he ensures that Verbal remains unpredictable.
During his patter about barbershop quartets in Skokie, Illinois, or working
on a coffee plantation in Guatemala, Spacey sometimes strikes the kind of
absent-minded self-amusement that registers convincingly as memory.
Verbal is only a conman but he enjoys the con. Spacey suggests the
pleasure Verbal finds in his work of misdirection.

In each of the flashback sequences, Singer finds ways to mark his
character's hidden significance. Verbal is the first suspect to enter the
lineup room – singled out with a lingering close-up on his crippled leg – a
visual marker of his difference from the others. He is the last to speak the
required line in the lineup. Spacey underplays, allowing his body language
to speak, not objecting, not even bristling, always keeping something in
reserve, but never seeming less than intelligent, especially when admitting
to being stupid. In contrast, all the other suspects, even Keaton to some
extent, bubble over with attitude, jockeying for ascendancy, bluffing,
cursing, joking, threatening – roosters in a barnyard empty of chickens.
Whatever voice of reflection there is in the film is his. However, in
retrospect Spacey's sub-Dostoevskian performance is effective exactly to
the degree to which one can believe in meekness as a strategy, as a covert
representation of the aspiration to absolute power. Singer is particularly
keen on exploiting Spacey's mercurial capacity to play emotional

Another clue

contradictions without missing a beat: 'He looks kind of peevish and wimpy. Audiences feel sorry for him. But one second he can look terrifying and the next second he can look completely innocent.'[48]

In this respect, consider how Spacey portrays Verbal's reaction to the most extreme and visually stylised representation of the film's unrelenting portrayal of the male need for control at all costs – the Soze family massacre. It is through this scarcely credible act of violence that Soze achieves a mythic status throughout the global criminal underworld. Singer shoots this Soze – not in fact played by Spacey – with long flowing hair, so that he looks like an avenging angel. Deliberately or not, Singer enriches this sense of an expanding or perhaps sleight-of-hand (now you see him and now you don't) myth by allowing four different people to appear as Soze in the course of the film: Spacey, a stunt man, another actor and himself.[49] 'The greatest trick the devil ever pulled was convincing the world he didn't exist.' As this flashback ends, Verbal claims to believe in God: 'But the only thing I'm afraid of is Keyser Soze.' And when you examine the fear in Kevin Spacey's eyes as he says the line, you remain convinced Verbal is afraid of Keyser Soze. And that makes sense even after the first time you've seen the film. The only thing he's afraid of is himself: what he is capable of, to get his way, to stay on top, untouched. So, largely due to the subtlety of Spacey's performance, Verbal does not appear to be lying. Instead, it's as if he's warning the monomaniacal Kujan, who insists on seeing Keaton as Soze. In *The Usual Suspects*, no man speaks except to gain advantage over another man.

Singer's probing camera, which likes to start in a close-up on Spacey's face only to move even closer, treats male faces like question marks. I mentioned earlier that Verbal even says at one point (in a voiceover): 'A man can't change what he is – he can convince anyone he's someone else – but never himself.' The irony becomes obvious the second time around, but to what extent does Spacey's performance of this contradiction sharpen the irony? On subsequent viewings, the physical and emotional suffering that Spacey plays so acutely, the sense of a life carved out of a constant perception of limits, plays equally well as an awareness of the performance of male weakness as a refuge from the burden of power won through ceaseless vigilance and ruthlessness. However, with the Verbal/Keyser dynamic we move out of psychological realism and into a kind of pop Jacobean allegorical dualism.

Verbal's flashbacks are both confessional and investigative, but investigative with a twist: they are told to *prevent* the solution of a crime. Not only that, but Verbal's flashbacks gain enormously in credibility from his own often openly emotional reactions to them. These emotions and his range of responses to Kujan's threats credibly frame the flashbacks as confessional.[50]

If some details remain opaque then, that is because Keyser Soze escapes; evil escapes not just from the moral accountability of the narrative, but from the viewer's accountability, as well. It's this ultimate detachment of the force of active evil that blocks viewers from completely understanding the narrative (from being able to lay claim to control of the narrative, to the extent that knowledge and power overlap).

However, the discovery of unreliability does impose an intellectual task on the viewer. Nigel Andrews called *The Usual Suspects* the fast-food *Rashomon*.[51] (Whereas Kevin Pollak has said of the film's culinary appeal: 'It's a movie that makes you feel smart. It doesn't cater to you like so many movies do, like fast food.'[52]) Kurosawa's landmark *Rashomon*, with its series of narrators whose accounts contradict each other, imposed a similar burden. In *Rashomon*, the viewer discovers as soon as the narrative point of view shifts to another character that unreliability is an issue for understanding the truth of events. Anthony Asquith's whodunit, *The Woman in Question* (1950), also uses a series of partially overlapping and partially contradictory flashbacks by a number of characters. The detective who elicits this testimony is aware that each character's partiality undermines the reliability of what's said, and he sifts through their flashback statements to identify the killer. The viewer encounters undermined reliability within the unfolding of the genre conventions of *The Usual Suspects* when it's too late to participate in the challenge of re-interpretation while watching the film itself. The emotions inspired by the discovery effectively spill out of the dark space of the narrative into the comparative light of the everyday. The facts of the film are in the end not completely decipherable. They remain slightly out of grasp. This disturbance of the fit between story and understanding cannot be resolved – either in film or in reality. In interviews, Singer (invariably described as 'fast-talking') seems to prefer to sidestep this contradiction:

Finally, though, the story is everything: every scene, image, every line, every sound effect has to be related to something else in the story … You can go back to it two, three, four times and still say, 'Oh yeah, look at that! It's not just an aesthetic joke; it *means* something.'[53]

A precedent for the way in which that last scene upends the story's veracity may be instructive. Jean-Pierre Melville's crime film *Doulos the Finger Man* (1962) puts its audiences in a somewhat similar spot. Jean-Paul Belmondo plays Doulos as a brute who, upon discovering that his best friend is about to burgle a mansion on the outskirts of Paris, beats and eventually kills the man's girlfriend to find out the exact location of the robbery. He then promptly betrays his friend to the police. Though wounded by the police, Doulos's friend escapes and – barely pausing to recover – plots his revenge on Doulos. Meanwhile, Doulos uncovers his friend's buried cache of stolen loot from a murder/robbery committed at the beginning of the film. At last the two erstwhile friends and another comrade meet at a café. Doulos speedily retells the story. In a series of flashbacks, we see that from the first, Doulos was acting to protect his friend from being betrayed by his girlfriend. Doulos the betrayer is astonishingly transformed into Doulos the faithful – no less brutal, it is true, but loyalty and brutality are not conflicting traits.

Melville's handling of the narrative puts the viewer in the highly unsettling position of the friend who at first is certain he's been betrayed and then must reckon with the truth. The interpretation of two codes turns out to be at stake: the code of narrative and the elaborate code of male behaviour by which the underworld characters and even the police swear. When Doulos sets the story straight he redeems his honour. But his risky violent actions seemed to put that code in doubt. Behaviour is as open to misinterpretation as narrative. So certain of Doulos's betrayal was his friend that he has, disastrously enough, licensed a hit on Doulos – and at the end of the film risks and loses his own life in an attempt to prevent the murder being carried out. Ultimately, everyone pays the price for misunderstanding – and ends up dead.

In *Doulos*, flashbacks straighten out a story that's been twisted by the deceptions of perception. In *The Usual Suspects*, deceptive flashbacks turn out to be the way the master storyteller maintains his mastery over both the police and the credulous audience. In *The Usual Suspects*, the manipulation of power and the manipulation of narrative turn out to be correlated. The master storyteller is a betrayer – he betrays not only all the usual suspects – but the audience as well. Failing, in the last moments, to catch up with Soze, Kujan cannot redeem the narrative because it takes him too long to understand it. The story is over before the fictional world it has created can be set right side up again.

The audience is led to identify throughout with Kint's role as underdog, both within the flashbacks and during the unmerciful grilling by the cop, representative of society's rule of law. But Kujan, who is honest enough, is also depicted as being so obsessed with destroying bent cop Keaton that he refuses to believe that he's not dead and, a little later, not Keyser Soze. Elsewhere, Singer portrays the law almost unrelentingly as merciless, arrogant, violent, mostly corrupt and dead wrong. It's a bitter picture, even if it's a compelling one, playing to anti-authoritarian instincts in the audience. Every character is either a cop or a crook, with the exception of the one token woman – who is a lawyer! The striking narrowness of this social landscape handily reduces the question of moral choice to a formulaic black or white.

This doesn't quite explain why many viewers took pleasure in the 'betrayal' which Kint forces upon us as the final twist in the plot, when he reveals his 'true' identity. If one of the deeper pleasures of entertainment is its magical ability to reconcile the irreconcilable, Kint/Soze more than fills the bill. The duality of gimpiness and malevolence satisfyingly evokes the tension between the compulsory misery of everyday life and the compensatory fantasy of empowerment. A quick glimpse of that fantasy is all we need and about as much as narrative credibility can bear. Kint's ultimate transformation into Soze effectively delivers the audience from the domination of the narrative. Verbal, as storyteller, has manipulated the hell out of us. The bad guy and the audience escape together. The sound editing of the final sequence is an overlapping montage of audio cues, clues and lies, a last-moment attempt to rewrite and straighten out some of the manipulated twists of the narrative, while Verbal untwists his not really crippled body. Ordinarily, this kind of elaborate audio montage is ascribed to the confused consciousness of a single character, the hero or

The final betrayal

heroine, as he or she comes to grips with the truth. (The compulsive liar of *The Locket* [1946] is seized with just such an audio attack, her consciousness disintegrating as she walks up the aisle to her wedding.) This disjunctive montage seems at first so dedicated to Kujan, to whom that truth dawns. But it actually spills over the entire scene, generalising its effect so that it becomes clear that it's ascribed to the dawning consciousness of the audience. It ends with a repetition of Verbal's line that 'The greatest trick the devil ever pulled was convincing the world he didn't exist.' The last shot is a flashback to Verbal in the police station, his fingers to his lips: 'And poof, he's gone.'

This final appeal returns the film to the issue of invisibility with which it began. You can take it lightly – as a magic trick. Or you could say that the film is issuing a warning about a new invisible Satan abroad in the land. The mystery surrounding Keyser Soze's identity turns out to be coextensive with the mystery of who controls the narrative: we realise that the narration has been unreliable exactly at the point when we discover who Soze is. The strategy of unreliability turns out to be linked to the mythic figure of the trickster, who gleefully uses disguise, lying and the dirtiest of dirty tricks to gain control. The unmasked Soze has demonstrated that the varied configurations or principles of order that have been at stake throughout the movie – the law, the team, masculinity, the family, storytelling itself – have been found wanting, limiting, false or inhibiting. An interplay between a complex disjunctive soundtrack which replays the film as a tissue of lies is accompanied by the only chase scene in the film: the law fails to arrest the criminal just as our chase after narrative coherence proves to be an arresting failure. What's left is the unapologetic, unalloyed triumph of evil, if evil is synonymous with the principle of disorder, or with the impossibility of identification.

Notes

1 *Guardian*, 24 August 1995, p. 10.

2 'Writing *The Usual Suspects*', *Scenario*, Winter 1995, p. 51.

3 'Cinema: Dalya Alberge Talks to Bryan Singer', *The Times*, 24 August 1995, p. 11.

4 Joe Sharkey, *Death Sentence: The Inside Story of the John List Murders* (New York: Signet, 1990), p. 116.

5 John List's letter to his pastor is quoted in full in Timothy B. Benford and James P. Johnson, *Righteous Carnage: The List Murders* (New York: Scribners, 1991), pp. 267–9.

6 Sharkey, *Death Sentence*, p. 259. Details on the List segment of *America's Most Wanted*, pp. 255–61.

7 'Writing *The Usual Suspects*', p. 52.

8 Ibid., p. 53.

9 Sharkey, *Death Sentence*, p. 172.

10 Ibid., p. 124.

11 Siegfried Kracauer, *From Caligari to Hitler: A Psychological History of the German Film* (Princeton: Princeton University Press, 1947), p. 85.

12 *Guardian*, 29 November 1996, p. 11.

13 Frank Krutnick, *In a Lonely Street: Film Noir, Genre, Masculinity* (London: Routledge, 1991), p. 201. In discussing what he calls the 'caper film', he says, 'the group sets itself against the law and mainstream society, but its unity tends to be jeopardised by individual failings and often through a sexual lapse as with Emmerich (Louis Calhern) and the voyeuristic Doc (Sam Jaffe) in *The Asphalt Jungle*, and the weak and besotted George (Elisha Cook Jr) in *The Killers*' [sic: *The Killing*]. He does not consider the possibility that the all-male group could be implicitly constituted as a bulwark against female sexuality. The sexual lapses he adduces as examples occur after the work of the criminal group is over, i.e. at the point when individual psychology begins to overtake group psychology.

14 *Time Out*, 16 August 1995, p. 26.

15 *Guardian*, 24 August 1995, p. 10.

16 Polygram production information, *The Usual Suspects*, August 1995.

17 James Naremore, *More Than Night: Film Noir in Its Contexts* (Berkeley: University of California Press, 1998), p. 129.

18 'Writing *The Usual Suspects*', p. 192.

19 Ibid., p. 52.

20 Janet Maslin, 'Putting Guys Like That in a Room Together', *The New York Times*, 9 August 1995.

21 'Liane Bonin on Bryan Singer's *The Usual Suspects*', *Filmmaker*, Summer 1995, p. 31.

22 Ibid.

23 John Fried, 'The Usual Suspects', *Cineaste*, Summer 1996, p. 53.

24 See Ian Nathan and Mark Salisbury, 'Who the Hell Does Keyser Soze Think He Is?', *Empire*, September 1995, to get a flavour of the early interest.

25 Barbara Shulgasser, 'The Usual Suspects Steps Out of Lineup', *San Francisco Examiner*, 18 August 1995. Kenneth Turan, 'Frenzied Ride with Suspects', *Los Angeles Times*, 16 August 1995. Desson Howe, 'The Usual Suspects', *Washington Post*, 18 August 1995. Jack Kroll, 'Crooks, Creeps and Cons', *Newsweek*, 28 August 1995.

26 Roger Ebert, 'The Usual Suspects', *Chicago Sun-Times*, 18 August 1995.

27 Georgia Brown, 'Great Pretenders', *The Village Voice*, 22 August 1995.

28 Anthony Lane, 'The Big Roundup', *The New Yorker*, 14 August 1995.

29 A. O. Scott, 'Backward Reel the Grisly Memories', *The New York Times*, 15 March 2001.

30 Ibid.

31 Christopher Tookey, 'Tense Thriller Where the Plot Is the Chief Suspect', *The Daily Mail*, 25 August 1995, p. 40.

32 Foster Hirsch, *Detours and Lost Highways: A Map of Neo-Noir* (New York: Limelight Editions, 1999), p. 287.

33 Ibid.

34 Anthony Lane, 'The Big Roundup', p. 87.

35 Polygram production information, *The Usual Suspects*.

36 'Writing *The Usual Suspects*', p. 195.

37 David Kronke, 'Swimming with Alligator', *Los Angeles Times*, 13 August 1995.

38 Ira Nayman, 'The Man Who Wasn't There: Narrative Ambiguity in 3 Recent Hollywood Films', *Creative Screenwriting*, Spring 2001, p. 57.

39 Stanley Orr, 'Postmodernism, Noir, and *The Usual Suspects*', *Literature/Film Quarterly*, vol. 27 no. 1, 1999, p. 68.

40 'Writing *The Usual Suspects*', p. 195.

41 Krutnik, *In a Lonely Street*, p. 136.

42 *Guardian*, 24 August 1995, p. 10.

43 Richard Dyer 'Resistance through Charisma: Rita Hayworth and *Gilda*', in E. Ann Kaplan (ed.), *Women in Film Noir* (London: BFI, 1980), p. 91.

44 Naremore, *More Than Night*, pp. 221–3.

45 The final draft of McQuarrie's script is printed in *Scenario*, Winter 1995.

46 'Writing *The Usual Suspects*', p. 195.

47 'Nailing the Suspects', *Guardian*, 29 November 1996, p. 11, for both the last-minute decision and the quote.

48 Kronke, 'Swimming with Alligator'.

49 'Nailing the Suspects', p. 11.

50 Maureen Turim, *Flashbacks in Film* (London: Routledge, 1989), p. 172, spells out the two basic types of flashbacks in film noir.

51 Nigel Andrews, 'Fearful Five Play Deadly Charades', *Financial Times*, 24 August 1995, p. 15.

52 Nigel Floyd, 'Prime Suspects', *Time Out*, 16 August 1995, p. 27.

53 Geoff Andrew, 'Usual Suspects', *Time Out*, 16 August 1995, p. 26.

Credits

THE USUAL SUSPECTS

USA/Germany
1995

Director
Bryan Singer
Producers
Bryan Singer,
Michael McDonnell
Writer
Christopher McQuarrie
Director of Photography
Newton Thomas Sigel
Editor
John Ottman
Production Designer
Howard Cummings
Music
John Ottman

©Rosco Film GmbH & Bad
Hat Harry Productions, Inc

Production Companies
PolyGram Filmed
Entertainment and Spelling
Films International present
a Blue Parrot/Bad Hat Harry
production
Bryan Singer's film
Executive Producers
Robert Jones, Hans
Brockmann, François
Duplat, Art Horan
Co-producer
Kenneth Kokin
Production Supervisor
Vicky Herman
Production Accountant
Brian A. Williams
**Assistant Production
Accountant**
Lynn Hockin
Production Co-ordinator
Tom Adelman
**Assistant Production
Co-ordinator**
Douglas Morton
**NY Unit Production
Manager**
Jane Raab
Location Managers
Chanel Salzer,
Ashley Friedman
NY Unit:
Greg Schnabel
Location Assistant
Jun Lin
**Post-production
Supervisor**
Michael Tinger
**Post-production
Co-ordinator**
Jennifer Flynn

**Assistant to
Producers/Director**
Jennifer Flynn
**Assistants to the
Producers**
Yvette Brestyanszky,
Alexandra Schultze
Assistant to Mr Singer
Andrew Gorry
**Key Set Production
Assistant**
Matthew Eyraud
**Set Production
Assistants**
Deborah Tabak.
Michael Masumoto
**Office Production
Assistants**
Andrea Celandine Rice,
Josh Jaggers, Rachel Arno,
David Markland
**NY Unit Production
Assistant**
Brad Carroll
Interns
Scott Morgan, Luke Bittel
2nd Unit Director
Kenneth Kokin
1st Assistant Director
James Deck
2nd Assistant Director
Alan Steinman
**2nd 2nd Assistant
Director**
Athena Alexander
**NY Unit Assistant
Director**
Dave Marcellino

Script Supervisors
Wendy Dallas,
Haley McLane
2nd Unit:
Jana Ludwigova
Casting
Francine Maisler
Associates:
Kathy Driscoll, Lisa Miller
Extras:
TBS Casting
NY Unit Extras:
Judie Fixler
Additional Photography
Bruce Douglas Johnson
**2nd Unit Directors of
Photography**
Scott Sakamoto,
Eric Goldstein
1st Assistant Camera
Robert Carlson
2nd Unit:
Greg Kidd,
Lockwood J. Pierson
NY Unit:
Andrea Dorman
B Camera 1st Assistants
Baird Steptoe,
Mike Fauntleroy
2nd Assistant Camera
Richard Sobin
NY Unit:
Lance Rieck
Loaders
Amy Hergoth,
Paul DeMarte, Jad Carmona
Steadicam Operators
Scott Sakamoto,
Chris Squires

Key Grips
Joey DiAnda
NY Unit:
Steve Lynch
Best Boy Grip
Scott Patten
Dolly Grip
Bruce Hamme
Grips
Ken Beymer, Kevin Dean,
Shawn Ensign, Gregory
Franklin, Ross Guidici, Matt
Jackson, Richard Maxey,
William McDevitt, Daniel
McMahon, Linda Perry
Gaffers
Reinhart 'Rayteam' Peschke
2nd Unit:
Bob Amerian
Best Boy
David Gamerman
Electricians
Robert Bonilla, Arthur
Borquez, Craig Brink, Jim
Frohna, Michael Maahs,
Jerry Mandley,Michael
Parsons, Darrin Pullford,
Shawn Rhodes,
James Teiper
2nd Unit Electric
Mary Stankiewicz
Still Photographers
Linda Chen, Caroline
Burton, John Johnson
**Special Effects
Co-ordinator**
Roy Downey
Special Effects Foreman
Greg Hendrickson
Assistant Editor
Roger Fenton

Apprentice Editors
Kelley Pate, Andrew Gorry
Art Director
David Lazan
**Art Department
Co-ordinator**
Mark Meloccaro
Art Department PA
Lorri Wakefield
Set Decorator
Sara Andrews
Lead Scenic
Phillip Schneider
Scenic
Maria Jaramillo
Lead Person
Peter Borck
On-set Dresser
Francis Whitebloom
Storyboard Artist
John Coven
Shopper/Swing
Thomas Power
Swing
Joseph Grafmuller,
Steven Ingrassia
Prop Master
Tony Bonaventura
Assistant Props
Angel Acosta,
Scott Saunders
Set Construction Labour
William Bastiani, Charles
Billen Jr, Celia Parker,
Caroline Wallner, Ray
Poland, Liz Shaner,
Diane Taylor
Costume Designer
Louise Mingenbach

Costume Supervisor
Lori Eskowitz
Set Costumer
Tara Spurlock
Additional Costumer
Erin Beck
Costume Assistant
Caitlin Shamberg
NY Unit Wardrobe
Supervisor
Prudence Moriarty
Key Make-up
Michelle Bühler
Make-up Swing
Kimberly Greene
Special Effects Make-up
David Barton
Modus EFX Crew
Richard Mayberry, Chris
Cantley, Michele Barton,
David Greathouse,
Yolanda Squatpump
Key Hair
Barbara Olvera
Additional Make-up/Hair
Raqueli Dahan
Title Design
R.E.D. Productions
Opticals
Buena Vista Imaging
Colour Timer
Gloria Kaiser
Music
Conductor/Orchestrator/
Contractor
Larry Groupe
Assistant to Mr Ottman
Damon Intrabartolo
Music Editor
Lia Vollack

Music Recording/Mixing
Engineers
Darrell Harvey,
Dan Abernathy
Music Recorded/Mixed at
Studio West,
Rancho Bernard, CA
Soundtrack
"Le sons et les parfums
tournent dans l'air du soir"
by Claude Debussy,
performed by Jon Kull;
"Steppin' Out" by Paul
Nelson, Carl Verheyen,
performed by Paul Nelson
Sound Mixer
Geoffrey Patterson
Recordists
Jack Keller, David Behle
Boom Operator
Craig Woods
Re-recording Mixers
Robert Litt, Elliot Tyson,
Greg P. Russell
Re-recording Facility
Warner Hollywood Studios
Digital Layback
Supervisor
David B. Long
Supervising Sound
Editor
Chuck Michael
Sound Editing
Acme Soundworks
Assistant Sound Editors
Tricia Linklater, Paul Parsons
Negative Cutter
Mary Beth Smith
Dialogue Editors
David Spence,
Sukey Fontelieu

Sound Effects Editors
Nash Michael, Karen
Wilson, Richard Burton
ADR
Supervisor:
George Berndt
Co-ordinator:
Leigh French
Recordists:
Greg Steele, Rick Canelli
Mixers:
Charleen Richards,
Thomas J. O'Connell
Editor:
Donald Sylvester
Foley
Supervisor:
Mark Pappas
Artists:
Claudette Cucci,
John Cucci
Recordists:
Don Givens,
Tammy Treadwell
Mixers:
Randy Petroski,
Robert Deschaine
Editor:
Jonathan Klein
Marine Co-ordination
The Charter Connection,
Bertram McCann
Transportation
Co-ordinator
Geno Hart
Transportation Captains
Joe Cosentino, Ken Plumlee
Transportation
Co-captain
Joseph Aroesti

Transportation
Operations Manager
Ron Pope
Drivers
Michael Banlowe, Jody
Bingenheimer, Robin D.
Bishop, Joseph Cosentino,
Pat Cosentino, Sherri
Cosentino, Frances Culp,
Angel Desanti, Sean Dugan,
Antonio Franchi, Eugene
Farrington, Jerry Snajczuk,
Johnathon Gorman, Glenn
Knowlton, Mark McDermitt,
Jeff Moore, Steve Nikolai,
Randy Tenhaeff, William
Smallwood, Mike Welch,
David Wilson
Transportation
Picture Cars
Security
C.A.S.T. Security, Tony
Estrado; John Alvarez
Caterer
Mario's Catering
Craft Service
Ellen Francisco
First Aid
John Herget
Production Financing
Newmarket Capital Group,
L.P., Bank of America
**Finance & Distribution
Counsel**
George Sheanshang, Esq
Production Counsel
Alexander, Halloran,
Nau & Rose

**Completion Bond
Services**
Film Finances
**Scheduling & Budgeting
Software**
Screenplay Systems
Production Insurance
RHH/Albert G. Ruben
Stunt Co-ordinators
Gary Jensen
2nd Unit:
Ethan Jensen
Stunt Players
William Bates, Kenneth
Blazer, Fernando Celis,
Michael Carr, Ashley
Casino, John Casino,
Max Daniels, Joe Dunne,
Diamond Farnsworth,
Alex Gaona, John Gillespie,
Bob Havice, Bill Judkins,
Pat Millicano, Ryan Patrick
Ross, Harry Wowchuk
Stand-ins
Michael Bentley,
Johnny Tonini
Unit Publicist
David Pollick
Publicity
Baker Winokur Ryder
**Special thanks to the
following people for their
unwavering enthusiasm
and invaluable support in
making this film**
John Baer, Chris Ball, Mike
Berg, David Bloomfield,
Brandon Boyce, Lee Carroll
and Rex Neilson, Ames
Cushing, David Duncan,
Andrea Eastman, David B.

Feldman, Ilene Feldman,
George Freeman, Brian
Gersh, Katharine Goodman,
Mark Halloran, Joanne
Horowitz, Mitch Horwits,
Tracey Jacobs, Brian
Kingman, Michael Kuhn,
Dylan Kussman, Los
Angeles Mayor's Office -
Jonathan Roberts and Cody
Cluff, Pippa Markham, Jane
Moore, Adam Moos, Denis
Pregnolato, Russell
Schwartz, Grace Sinden,
Immanuel Spira, Nobert and
Mildred Singer, Kathryn
Smith, Jill Tandy, Stewart Till,
Will Tyrer, Victoria Wisdom

Cast
Stephen Baldwin
Michael McManus
Gabriel Byrne
Dean Keaton
Chazz Palminteri
Agent David 'Dave' Kujan
Kevin Pollak
Todd Hockney
Pete Postlethwaite
Kobayashi
Kevin Spacey
Roger 'Verbal' Kint
Suzy Amis
Edie Finneran
Giancarlo Esposito
Jack Baer
Benicio del Toro
Fred Fenster
Dan Hedaya
Sgt Jeffrey Rabin

Paul Bartel
smuggler
Carl Bressler
Saul Berg
Phillip Simon
Fortier
Jack Shearer
Renault
Christine Estabrook
Dr Plummer
Clark Gregg
Dr Walters
Morgan Hunter
Arkosh Kovash
Ken Daly
translator
Michelle Clunie
sketch artist
Louis Lombardi
Strausz
Frank Medrano
Rizzi

Ron Gilbert
Daniel Metzheiser
Vito D'Ambrosio
arresting officer
Gene Lythgow
cop on pier
Bob Elmore
bodyguard 1
David Powledge
bodyguard 2
Bob Pennetta
bodyguard 3
Bill Bates
bodyguard 4
Smadar Hanson
Keyser's wife
Castula Guerra
Arturro Marquez
Peter Rocca
Arturro's bodyguard
Bert Williams
old cop

[uncredited]
Peter Greene
Redfoot

9,518 feet
105 minutes

Dolby SRD
Colour by
Foto-Kem Laboratory
Prints by
Technicolor
2.35:1 [Super 35]
MPAA: 33466

Credits compiled by
Markku Salmi,
BFI Filmographic Unit

Also Published

L'Argent
Kent Jones (1999)

Blade Runner
Scott Bukatman (1997)

Blue Velvet
Michael Atkinson (1997)

Caravaggio
Leo Bersani & Ulysse Dutoit
(1999)

Crash
Iain Sinclair (1999)

The Crying Game
Jane Giles (1997)

Dead Man
Jonathan Rosenbaum
(2000)

Don't Look Now
Mark Sanderson (1996)

Do the Right Thing
Ed Guerrero (2001)

Easy Rider
Lee Hill (1996)

The Exorcist
Mark Kermode (1997,
2nd edn 1998)

Independence Day
Michael Rogin (1998)

Last Tango in Paris
David Thompson (1998)

**Once Upon a Time in
America**
Adrian Martin (1998)

Pulp Fiction
Dana Polan (2000)

The Right Stuff
Tom Charity (1997)

**Saló or The 120 Days of
Sodom**
Gary Indiana (2000)

Seven
Richard Dyer (1999)

The Silence of the Lambs
Yvonne Tasker (2002)

The Terminator
Sean French (1996)

Thelma & Louise
Marita Sturken (2000)

The Thing
Anne Billson (1997)

**The 'Three Colours'
Trilogy**
Geoff Andrew (1998)

Titanic
David M. Lubin (1999)

Trainspotting
Murray Smith (2002)

The Wings of the Dove
Robin Wood (1999)

**Women on the Verge of a
Nervous Breakdown**
Peter William Evans (1996)

**WR – Mysteries of the
Organism**
Raymond Durgnat (1999)